The
Liturgy
after the
Liturgy

The *Liturgy* after the Liturgy

Mission and Witness from an Orthodox Perspective

ION BRIA

WCC Publications, Geneva

Cover design: Stephen Raw
Cover photo: Peter Williams

ISBN 2-8254-1189-2

© 1996 WCC Publications, World Council of Churches,
150 route de Ferney, 1211 Geneva 2, Switzerland

Printed in the Netherlands

Table of Contents

Introduction vii

1. The World of the Liturgy 1

2. The Liturgy after the Liturgy 19

3. Ecumenical Orientations in Liturgy 36

4. Gospel and Culture and Liturgy 44

5. Liturgy and Common Christian Witness 55

6. The Spectrum of Orthodoxy 65

7. The Dynamics of Liturgy in Mission 83

Introduction

The perception is widespread that the Orthodox churches are predominantly "liturgical" churches, concentrating on ritual and hierarchy and neglecting theological research, especially that pertaining to the church's calling as a movement for mission. Furthermore, according to this line of thought, since the Orthodox have neither experiences of nor perspectives on mission, they have little to contribute to the ecumenical debate on these issues.

However, the World Council of Churches has understood from the beginning that the Orthodox do have their own theological tradition regarding mission and that involving this tradition in the ecumenical dialogue on mission can make for greater depth and completeness. At the beginning of the 1970s, when critical dissonances in the missiological debate were becoming sharper and the urgency of an holistic articulation of mission was increasingly evident, the WCC encouraged the Orthodox churches to become more active in this discussion and to articulate their position in an ecumenical framework.

Consequently, since the WCC's world mission conference on "Salvation Today" (Bangkok 1972-73), Orthodox theologians from both Eastern and Oriental Orthodox churches have met on several occasions to reflect on the elements of a missiological typology of the Orthodox churches. The typology proposed corresponds to the history of their own mission and especially to the constant tradition in which worship and liturgy are an essential factor of proclaiming and confessing Christ. We call this typology the "liturgy after the liturgy". Rather than analyzing the Orthodox insights into missiology as such, for which *martyria* remains the decisive concept, we are concerned with the missiological grounds on which the liturgy after the liturgy could be approached.

As the Orthodox have been stimulated over the past two decades to formulate their principles and perspectives on mission, evangelism and common witness, a rich and diverse literature has arisen; and the presentation in this book draws upon materials produced by Orthodox theologians as contributions to the WCC's major mission conferences since the one in Bangkok: the Melbourne conference (1980) and the San Antonio conference (1989).

More crucial than the question of what "mission" really means for the Orthodox is the question of how the historic Orthodox churches should engage in mission within the complex reality of the present generation, especially after the social and political upheavals in Central and Eastern Europe. In the latter chapters of this book we explore some facets of this question.

The wider context of this exploration is an ecumenical situation in which many churches, including WCC members, are saying that visible unity is unattainable and the search for unity is thus misplaced. Ecumenism, these voices suggest, should focus on building good relations across denominational lines. Many continue to ignore the essential connections between mission, unity and renewal, between personal relations and the global unity of all Christians. We must recover the challenge posed to the churches since the beginning of the ecumenical movement: to seek visible unity in order to be able to engage in mission and evangelism together. To remain complacent about the historic divisions among the churches means to undermine the mission of the church.

I hope that this book will in some way help to encourage the ecumenical movement and the World Council of Churches, through its various programmes, to continue to facilitate in-depth encounters between Orthodox and other WCC member churches, not only to compare missionary ideas and strategies, but also to envisage possible connections and pairings among these Christian traditions, so that they will overcome their missiological ignorance of one another, which amounts to both lack of knowledge and lack of pastoral care for one another as Christian bodies.

ION BRIA

1. The World of the Liturgy

The word "liturgy" (Latin *liturgia*) comes from the Greek *leitourgia*, which is in turn derived from the words *leitos* (public, from *laos*, people) and *ergon* (work). In the ancient vocabulary of Christian worship it refers specifically to the celebration of the eucharist by a local community, under the ministry of a consecrated priest, on Sunday, the day of the Lord.

Through the offering of the gifts of bread and wine and their consecration in the body and blood of Jesus Christ, the eucharistic liturgy commemorates Christ's incarnation, sacrifice on the cross and resurrection. The celebrant and the faithful then share these consecrated gifts as holy communion. The eucharist represents our redemption in Jesus Christ and its conclusion in the coming of the Holy Spirit on the church. But it is not just a commemorative festival; the eucharistic liturgy "actualizes" the redemptive ministry of Jesus Christ in sharing his own body and blood with the baptized faithful. The body and blood of Christ are the true food and drink of the church; and the role of the eucharistic liturgy is to create, nurture and sustain the *koinonia* of the church.

St Paul refers to the institution of the Lord's supper (1 Cor. 11:23-26) on the night when Jesus was betrayed (Matt. 26:26-28; Mark 14:22-24; Luke 22:17-20; cf. John 6:32-58); and several references in the Acts of the Apostles point to the practice of eucharistic communion (cf. 2:42,46; 20:7). In his first *Apology* (c. 140) Justin Martyr transmits the basic structure of the post-apostolic eucharistic liturgy. The structure and language have varied according to generations, places, confessions and cultures,[1] but within this diversity there is a core of symbolic rites for the consecration of the gifts and the communion of the faithful. The best-known liturgy is that of St John Chrysostom (c. 347-407), which is of Antiochian origin.[2] The Orthodox also use the liturgy of St Basil the Great (c. 330-390) and the Office of the Presanctified Gifts ascribed to Gregory Dialogos, bishop of Rome (c. 540-604).

Over the years the meaning of *leitourgia* has gone far beyond the Sunday eucharistic celebration and communion,[3] for example in the monastic practice of daily celebration of eucharist. A clear distinction is also to be made between the eucharistic liturgy and rituals for non-sacramental church services and prayers. While the latter also convey a profound doctrinal and theological content and have taken on a certain uniformity and universality in Orthodox churches, they do vary more than the eucharistic liturgy; and modifying, expanding and proposing new texts for such services to meet the pastoral needs of the faithful is the continuing responsibility of each local church.

As the background for examining the impact of the liturgy on mission, spirituality and diakonia, we begin with a brief sketch of the main parts of the liturgy of St John Chrysostom.[4]

The order of the liturgy

The first part, the liturgy of the word (also called the liturgy of the catechumens, because those who were preparing for baptism were allowed to be present for it) brings to memory the coming of Christ and the beginning of his ministry. The opening doxology of the Holy Trinity signifies both that Christ dedicated himself to God from the beginning, as he later offered the gifts to his Father, and that it was through the incarnation that humankind first learned that God is three persons. The service continues with a great litany, a series of petitions, not only for the church but for the "whole world", because Christians know that their God is the Lord of all, to which the people respond, "*Kyrie, eleison*" ("Lord, have mercy").

During the third of the three antiphons which follow, the deacon or priest, surrounded by acolytes, carries the book of the gospels from the altar through the nave in the midst of the people (the "little entrance"), showing it to them, for the gospel represents Christ who appeared to the multitude. The book of the gospels, which is always on the altar and is frequently displayed, is a token of God's presence in the world. The little entrance thus symbolizes the incarnation, Christ's mission and message, his death on the cross and his resurrection, which sanctify the faithful.

The New Testament readings, which recognize the identity of the new people of God by proclaiming the message in a common language, are taken from the Acts of the Apostles or the epistles and from the gospels. The reading of the epistle is introduced by the hymn of *trisagion*: "O holy God, holy and strong, holy and immortal, have mercy on us." The church professes again the unity of God and the Trinity, showing the harmony between Old and New Testaments. The angels and worshipping community form a single choir, one church. The gospel text is explained in the homily, an exegetical sermon. The litany of "fervent supplication" and the litany of the catechumens then conclude this first part of the service.

Central to the second part of the liturgy is the ritual leading to the consecration of the bread and wine. It takes place between the *prothesis*

— the offertory table, where the simple elements acquire the new characteristic of becoming an offering, representing our Lord during the first phase of his life on earth — and the altar table. To prepare for the celebration of eucharist the priest, in unity with the congregation, raises his hands and prays to be considered worthy to perform this act without sin, although "none is worthy... to draw near and minister to you, O King of glory".

The preparation of the elements for consecration represents Christ's suffering and death. The whole of the offertory, in which the gifts are offered both in thanksgiving to God for what we have received and in supplication for blessings yet to come, commemorates those events which denote Christ's human weakness — his suffering, crucifixion and death — without which humankind could not be redeemed. During this ritual, the bread receives the capacity to be offered to God, but it remains bread, typifying the Lord's body in his early years, for he himself was an offering from his birth onwards.

The great entrance is a solemn procession of the offerings through the nave of the church. In the midst of the church, facing the congregation, the priest prays God to remember the faithful in his kingdom, then places the chalice and the paten (disk) on the table inside the altar. After the choir has sung the "cherubic hymn" ("... let us put away all earthly care, so that we may receive the King of all, invisibly escorted by the angelic hosts..."), the priest prepares himself and those present for the offertory. He recites a prayer in which he confesses the difference between the ministry of a "sinful and unworthy servant" and the priesthood of Jesus Christ, who is the real celebrant ("for you are both he that offers and he that is offered").

After the *"ectenia* of oblation", which includes a petition for forgiveness of our sins, the priest and the congregation wish peace to each other. Introducing the confession of faith, the priest urges the faithful, "Let us love one another that with one mind we may confess the Father and the Son and the Holy Spirit, Trinity consubstantial and undivided." This love is manifested in the kiss of peace, when the priests embrace each other, saying "Christ is in the midst of us; he is and ever shall be". Here is the biblical vision of the catholicity of God's community: in our communion with one another, rooted in the experience of Christ, we are sharing God's all-embracing communion. The creed which is then confessed is the summary of the doctrines of the Christian faith as formulated in the fourth century by the first and second ecumenical councils (Nicea 325 and Constantinople 381).

4   *The Liturgy after the Liturgy*

The heart of the liturgy is constituted by the *anaphora*, the "lifting up" of the offering and of our hearts. This begins with the blessing ("the grace of our Lord Jesus Christ..."), the invitation ("let us give thanks to the Lord") and the hymn "Holy, holy, holy is the Lord God of Sabaoth". The preface makes clear that "the night that he was betrayed" was the night "in which he did give himself for the life of the world". The words of institution ("take, eat...; drink of it all of you...") are followed by the *anamnesis* ("remembering... all those things which came to pass for our sakes..."). With the consecration of the offerings, the priest lifts up the paten and the chalice, saying "Thine own, of thine own, we offer unto thee in all and for all". The word "eucharist" now has the double meaning of both thanksgiving and sacrifice.

The *anaphora* continues with the *epiklesis*, a prayer of invocation to God to "send down thy Holy Spirit upon us and upon these gifts here set forth" and "make this bread the precious body of Christ and that which is in this cup the precious blood of thy Christ". The transformation is thus in the power of the Holy Spirit. With this prayer, the offerings are consecrated and sanctified; the sacrifice is complete. After the prayer of sanctification the *anaphora* concludes with a commemoration of the Virgin Mary, the Mother of God, and intercessions for the local bishop and for prophets, apostles, saints and civil authorities.

In the *ectenia* before the Lord's prayer and in preparation for holy communion, the priest prays especially for the "unity of the faith and the communion of the Holy Spirit..., calling to remembrance all the saints". The priest and congregation then say the Lord's prayer, ending with the doxology and the sign of the cross. This is followed by a prayer invoking Christ to give himself by his own hand to the priest and the people.

During the *prothesis* (the preparation of the elements which generally takes place before the liturgy), a square piece has been cut from the round leavened loaf (*artos*), in which are inscribed the letters IC XC NI KA (the Greek means "Jesus Christ conquers"). This piece is called the *amnos*, holy Lamb or holy bread. The priest now lifts this *amnos*, saying, "The holy gifts for the holy people of God", and breaks it into four parts, saying, "The Lamb of God is broken and divided; broken but not divided; always eaten and never consumed; but sanctifying them that partake". The part which bears the letters IC is then dropped into the chalice, and warm water (*zeon*) is poured into the chalice, symbolizing the descent of the Holy Spirit on the church. The priest partakes of the piece marked XC; and the two pieces marked NI and KA are placed into the chalice for the communion of the people, to which the priest invites the congregation, saying, "With the fear of God, with faith and with love, draw near". The priest then prays, "O God, save thy people and bless thine inheritance."

Following the communion, the dismissal prayers ("O Lord, who blesses those that bless thee...") are introduced with the words "go forth in peace". The final benediction refers also to the intercessions and prayers of the fathers of the church and the saints. At the close of the liturgy, the priest gives the people *antidoron*, the remains of the bread from which the part to be consecrated has been left out. This commemorates the *agape* of the first Christians.

The essentials of the liturgy

Explaining some of the essential aspects of this liturgical schema could help to deepen the eucharistic understanding even of those churches which do not follow this form of the rite.

The most significant characteristic of the liturgy is its Christocentric character as part of an explicitly trinitarian theology. All the prayers, rituals and symbols, which are taken from biblical texts, make Christological affirmations which relate to the Trinity as a whole.

The gathering of the people in the presence of God the Trinity underscores the relational element. The *Pantocrator* is neither an absent and passive eternal being nor an all-powerful monitor of the sinful world ever ready to condemn the sinner. Here is a living God, the Father, who reveals his intimate relation with Jesus Christ: "You are my son, the Beloved" (Mark 1:11). At the same time, the liturgy discloses God's plan of redemption of all, not only the church, but also the world. The sanctuary, the holy place of Christians, is joined to the narthex, the avenue into the world.

The liturgy is not just a commemoration of Christ's ministry to the world, teaching, healing, feeding the people; it is the realization, in each new context, of the history of the world, of "what the Lord has done" (Psalm 64:8). The faithful can see with their eyes and hear with their ears and hearts the message of the gospel in the symbolic language of Jesus. Through the icons, which stand for the communion of saints, "the heavens are torn apart" (Mark 1:10). Again, this is a matter not just of visualizing the Word of God, but also of partaking the Body of Christ for the forgiveness of sins and for eternal life.

The connection with God's plan of redemption gives all liturgical services their Christocentric dimension. In the words of Cabasilas:

> It is Christ himself, in his capacity as priest, who set apart the body of the Lord, offered it up, took it to himself and consecrated it to God, and who sacrificed it. It is the Son of God in person who separated himself from the mass of humankind; it is he who has offered himself to God... That is why the bread which is to be changed into his body is separated from the rest of the loaves by the priest.[5]

We offer bread and wine as symbols of mortal human life, and God gives us in return the living bread, the chalice of eternal life. In exchange for our offering, God accepts our bread and wine and gives us his own Son.

The consecration and transformation of the elements into the body of the Lord can be effective only by invoking the power of the Holy Spirit through prayer:

> It is the tradition of the fathers, who received this teaching from the apostles and from their successors, that the sacraments are rendered effective through prayer... None of the apostles or teachers of the church has ever appeared to say that they are sufficient to consecrate the offering of sacraments.[6]

The invocation of the Holy Spirit is not only for the consecration and transformation of the elements, but also for the fulfilment, the final effects of the work of redemption. Thus, Cabasilas says, the effect of Christ's teaching, ministry and death "considered in relation to ourselves" is "nothing other than the descent of the Holy Spirit upon the church":

> For the mysteries also represent the church, which is the Body of Christ; she received the Holy Spirit after our Lord's ascension; now she receives the gift of the Holy Spirit after the offerings have been accepted at the heavenly altar; God, who has accepted them, sends us the Holy Spirit in return..., for then and now there is one Mediator and one Spirit.[7]

The christological and ecclesiological dimensions of the liturgy are in accord with the understanding of the one God as communion of the Holy Trinity, which shapes every reality: prayer, ethics, mission, diakonia. Unity arises from a profound experience of the Holy Trinity. A growing ecumenical theological consensus affirms the trinitarian understanding of God as the basis for ecclesial life, which is why church unity cannot be reduced to an issue of organizational structure.[8]

The liturgy is called "eucharist" (from the Greek *eucharistia*, thanksgiving) because the liturgical community thankfully commemorates the whole assembly of saints:

The saints are the cause for which the church gives thanks to God. It is for them that she offers to him a spiritual sacrifice in thanksgiving; above all, it is for the blessed Mother of God, who surpasses all others in holiness. That is why the priest asks for nothing on behalf of the saints; rather, he asks that he may be assisted by them in his prayers...; for them the gifts are offered not in supplication but in thanksgiving.[9]

Those who are striving for perfection but have not yet reached it still need prayer; nevertheless, the priest calls them holy too:

Nothing prevents them from being sanctified by partaking of the holy mysteries, and from this point of view being saints. It is in this sense that the whole church is called holy, and that the apostle, writing to the Christian people as a whole, says to them, "Holy brethren, partakers of the heavenly calling" [Heb. 3:1]. The faithful are called saints because of the holy thing of which they partake, because of him whose body and blood they receive... If we should cut ourselves off, if we should separate ourselves from the unity of this most holy body, we partake of the holy mysteries in vain, for life cannot flow into dead and amputated limbs.[10]

Receiving the communion properly thus requires the unity of the faith and the communion of the Holy Spirit:

When our Lord with his cross battered down the wall of separation between God and ourselves, he saw that we who were separated had nothing in common with which to bridge the gap; the descent of the Holy Spirit upon the apostles achieved this. Since that time the fount of all graces has been opened for men by holy baptism, and, as St Peter says, we are made partakers of the divine nature [2 Pet. 1:4]. Therefore, he who wishes to commend himself to God and to place himself in his keeping has need of an unshakable faith and the aid of the Holy Spirit. Nor do we commend ourselves alone to God, but each other also; for, according to the law of charity, we must seek the good of others as well as our own.[11]

Two specific points are worth exploring here in somewhat greater detail: the meaning of the koinonia of the Holy Spirit and tradition as the celebration of the gospel.

Fellowship in the Spirit

The feast of Holy Trinity falls on the Monday after Pentecost in the liturgical calendar of the Eastern Christian tradition. This is an example of the close link that is always made between commemorating a biblical event and remembering the persons at the centre of that event. Pentecost emphasizes that nothing in God is impersonal; everything is personal. In the incarnation it is the Son of God who is manifested; at Pentecost the Spirit *as divine person* descended on the apostles and the community in Jerusalem.[12]

Writing to the Galatians about the authentic Christian life as a disciplined way of life which excludes radical contradictions, St Paul poses a series of questions (3:1-5) to underscore that they had received the Spirit not by doing "the works of the law" but by believing in the message of Jesus Christ crucified. Therefore, he says, "if we live by the Spirit, let us also be guided by the Spirit" (5:25). Christians must live and practise their faith in a new order or discipline totally organized by the Spirit of God, who not only brings into our lives the sense of divine presence and vitality but also regulates our day-to-day journey. The Spirit modifies the course of our life, perhaps even restructuring or dismantling its whole system to create a new one.

The promise of Jesus Christ that when the Spirit comes "he will guide you into all the truth" (John 16:23) was fulfilled at Pentecost. According to St John, the Spirit glorifies Jesus Christ by taking what belongs to him and declaring it to Christians (v.14). The Holy Spirit is the Spirit of truth because the Holy Spirit belongs to the communion of the Trinity and was sent to confirm what Jesus did for our salvation.

By communicating the life of God as it was realized in the life of Jesus Christ, who creates his own people according to God's will, the Spirit of truth places us within both the inner mystical life of God and the real history of the incarnated Logos. Everyone has his or her own spirituality which reflects a personal identity shaped in communion and solidarity with others; and the Spirit helps us to discover our own personality within communion with God.

To be sure, the doctrine of the Holy Spirit can be fertile soil for the growth of theological speculation and spiritual illusion. The Spirit who comes from God (cf. 1 John 4:1-3) can easily be given various false incarnations and false names. At a time when the need for true fellowship to regulate personal spirituality is more and more evident, people are appealing to the Holy Spirit to highlight individual salvation and private mystical experiences and to justify withdrawing into private ghettos, intolerant of those whose style of life is different. The Spirit may be invoked by one side or the other in domestic difficulties and ecclesiastical power struggles, forgetting St Paul's appeal not to model ourselves on the behaviour of the world around (cf. Rom. 12:2).

We have only begun to develop an understanding of what the koinonia of the Holy Spirit implies for the fellowship sought in the ecumenical movement. The expressions of ecumenical fellowship must constantly be explored and examined in terms of whether the way of communion in the Spirit is being prepared and realized. What are the keys of this fellowship?

The dynamic according to which the koinonia of the Spirit is realized is quite different from human alliances and covenants made in order to protect one's own self-interest by setting up barriers, divisions and discrimination. In the name of the Spirit who has no flesh and bones, the humanity of people with real flesh and bones has often been suppressed. The Holy Spirit whom Christians confess is a personal God who recognizes the value and meaning of each person, each community, each nation, each people. But our efforts to overcome unjust social and political orders and to renew the creation risk becoming negative and destructive if they are not grounded in the sanctification of the heart, where everyone has his or her own light. Our strength in identifying and tackling the external "root causes" of these problems may avail little if we are weak in reconstructing our own inner image according to the call of the Spirit to be perfect as God is perfect.

Not that there are precise criteria for measuring collaboration with the Holy Spirit. But in times of despair and death the Spirit helps us to raise our head and to come to hope and life. The Spirit constitutes the force of our wisdom and our weakness; our freedom and responsibility and the grace of the Spirit are "like a pair of wings".[13] As heavenly Comforter and Sustainer the Spirit never ceases to teach us, guide us and support us, openly or secretly. When our flesh and bones tremble, we say with St Paul, "We live in the Spirit".

Remembering and handing on

The liturgy shows that the mystery of Christ and the truth of the good news are beyond our concepts and creeds. The most appropriate way to experience and communicate the message is to celebrate the faith through doxological hymns and prayers and sacramental symbolism.

Since its very beginning the church has been called to "remember" the key events and key words in the history of salvation, to hand on the gospel by pointing back to the incarnation and ahead to the second coming. To this same process of "tradition" belong proclamation and memorial. Prayer, worship and communion have always formed the context for the witness of faith, including evangelism, mission and church life. The missionary structures were built on the liturgy of the word and the sacraments; and since the beginning the great variety of liturgies and rites, creeds and confessions has been due to the diversity of missionary contexts.

For the purposes of instructing the faithful and protecting the true faith from heresy, the church has always tended to limit the message to a few dogmas, articles of faith and confessional creeds, which serve as basic unifying factors of the Christian community. At the same time, a process of interpreting the gospel is always going on in every concrete historical, cultural and social setting. Whenever a new situation makes the content of the gospel unclear or even meaningless to people, it is necessary to identify the authentic continuity of the tradition in history. But this is not just a matter of dogmatic statements and doctrinal assertions. Tradition also implies a mode of existence. Obedience to the word of God cannot be separated from personal sanctification and love and service to humankind (cf. 1 Pet. 1:14f.), because the Logos both proclaims "the words of eternal life" (John 6:68) and is partaken as "the bread of life" (v.35).

How then does the celebration of the liturgy generate hope and become a real message in the face of problems for which one cannot find answers in the past? What is the "spirituality" that is proposed and determined in celebrating the liturgy today? The church fathers considered the present time as the "workshop of eschatology", that is, preparation for the age to come. The church has to struggle for the fulfilment of that history which was promised by God to all human beings and creation. It is constantly giving an account of how the kingdom is or is not within itself. The liturgical *epiklesis* is a powerful petition for the continuous presence of the Holy Spirit upon the earth. Having made this invocation we cannot avoid asking such questions as what sanctification means in terms of ecology and human rights.

The contemporary crisis of faith can hide the crisis of subjectivity and personal integrity. Orthodox Christians in particular may deceive themselves, covering up the crisis of faith with the sumptuous spectacle and formality of liturgy. But there is no salvation in us or in our ceremonies. The liturgy itself in fact counters such misunderstanding and misuse, for it implies an attitude of constant personal repentance and provides the means for this. It portrays the growth of faith in terms of finding a wedding garment for a sinful and unworthy servant — to use the imagery of the *troparia* in the office of preparation for holy communion:

> How may I, unworthy as I am,
> Enter into the brightness of thy saints?

> For if I come boldly to the king's palace
> My apparel doth convict me,
> In that I have no wedding garment,
> And I shall be bound and cast away by the angels.
> O Lord, cleanse my soul from all filthiness,
> And save me, for thou art loving-kind.

"Looking at all times for my conversion", the faithful recognize that they are altogether unworthy and ask God to accept "the repentance of a transgressor". Thus they confess, "You are the God of those who repent and the saviour of sinners."

The prayers for holy communion call to mind examples of people accepted because of their faith: the prostitute, the thief crucified alongside Jesus, the tax-collectors, the woman who was a sinner, the woman who anointed his feet, the prodigal son. Jesus Christ himself, who is the model of faith, did not disdain sitting at table with sinners in the house of Simon and received those who came at the eleventh hour. Against the background of the mystical intimacy with Christ offered at the eucharist, Judas remains the symbol of the "unworthy servant": "For I will not speak of the mystery to thine enemies, nor will I give thee a kiss like Judas; but like the thief I will acknowledge thee: Remember me, O Lord, in thy kingdom."

The liturgy itself also corrects the false assumption that the sacraments depend on the skill and musical artistry of the celebrants. Behind the rites and gestures the celebrants also need to believe in the mercy of God. In the *anaphora* of the liturgy of St Basil the Great, they refer to themselves as "thy sinful and unworthy servants whom thou hast suffered to minister at thy hallowed altar, not for our righteousness, for we have done no good thing on earth, but for thy mercy and the bounties which thou hast shed on us abundantly."

The "vertical" dimension of the liturgy is grounded in the recognition of the transcendence of God, "whose divine nature is inconceivable and glory incomprehensible, whose mercy to human beings is immeasurable and tenderness unspeakable". Something is *given* in the liturgy: the blessings of God, which belong to "the life of the world to come". Yet the strong emphasis in the present form of the liturgy on the "objective" conditions of salvation should not lead to the impression that the people's participation is limited and passive,[14] or that the liturgy is reserved for an initiated minority. In worship, personal identity is affirmed in the context of the communion of saints. The celebrant receives "names" for commemoration and prays by name for those who bring the gifts. In the liturgical experience, the faithful must discover both their spiritual roots and their relation to a community. Here is a sharp critique of the liturgical marketplace offered by television, where the homily becomes a lecture, prayer is only a matter of words and the faithful are consigned to silence. The mass media may create horizontal emotion but never vertical depth or ascent.

Spiritual discoveries

The work of the Lord and the work of the servants

The liturgical act represents the flowing together of the priesthood of Christ, as the only mediator between God and human beings, and the priesthood of his servants: the celebrants and the faithful:

> Even if it is true that Christ performs the sacrifice, we cannot attribute everything that is said and done throughout the liturgy to him. He alone accomplishes the special work and purpose of the liturgy — the consecration of the offerings and the sanctification of the faithful; but the prayers, supplications and demands which surround these rites are the acts of the priest. The first are the works of the Lord, the rest the work of servants; the latter prays, while the former answers prayer. The Saviour gives, and the priest offers thanks for what has been given; the priest offers, and the Lord accepts what is offered.[15]

Eucharist therefore is not simply a gift from God, something which God gives to us; God imparts himself, his very life. The bread of life is God himself living. God acts in each of his "mysteries", his sacraments. He purifies us in baptism, reshaping to its original form the human being who was corrupted by sin. He anoints us, giving the seal and assurance of the Holy Spirit. He feeds his people in order that they may become his body.

Facing the sins of the people

In the liturgy we are seeking forgiveness of sins and the inheritance of the kingdom: "For pardon and remission of our sins and transgressions, let us entreat the Lord." Sin is not only the absence of good but the brutality of evil. It has a real existence beyond humanity and history — "the authorities..., the cosmic powers of this present darkness..., the spiritual forces of evil in the heavenly places" (Eph. 6:12).

There are two facets to restoring integrity and drawing men and women out of bondage to evil and corruption. On the one hand, the liturgy speaks of "granting us in this world knowledge of thy truth". It was the will of the devil to keep humanity ignorant of God and of the divine plan and promise. The liturgy speaks of the word of God, revealing the mystery of God which has "turned us from the deceit of idols" and "brought us unto knowledge of thee, the true God and Father". Before the communion the believer promises, "I will not reveal your mystery to your adversary"; in other words, not to become intimate with the devil by telling him the secrets of God and thus to become powerful and knowledgeable, with the help of the faithful, against the will of "the God of ineffable mysteries, in whom are hidden the treasures of wisdom and knowledge".

On the other hand, the liturgy hallows a God who is gracious and full of compassion, whose Son humbled himself for our salvation, "giving himself as a ransom unto death, wherein we were held, sold under sin". The constant prayer "have mercy upon us" indicates the brokenness, danger and distress of the human condition; yet it is precisely people in this condition whom the liturgy invites to lift up their lives, symbolized in the gifts, and to present them on the heavenly altar, trusting that the compassionate God will "in turn send upon us divine grace and the gift of the Holy Spirit".

Both the celebrant and the faithful are in the same sinful condition; both need to repent in prayer: "Forgive me all my trespasses, voluntary and involuntary, and withhold not because of my sins the grace of the Holy Spirit from the gifts here set forth."[16]

The way to reconstitute the human being, created in God's "image and likeness", is to share the body which is broken and the blood which is shed for the forgiveness of sins. This is the heart of the New Testament. Here Christians are praying for a "sinless day" — which is a human impossibility — and for the "forgiveness and remission of our sins and transgressions". Partaking of the sacrament is not permitted to all (and not all are invited to communion), but only those who are worthy to receive it appropriately. But, as we saw earlier, the invitation "holy things to the holy" does not apply only to those who have attained perfection, but also to those "who are striving for it without having yet obtained it":

> Members of his Body, flesh of his flesh and bone of his bone, as long as we remain united to him, we live by holiness, drawing to ourselves, through the holy mysteries, the sanctity which comes from that Head and that Heart.[17]

This is why it is necessary for the church to identify new saints, not only martyrs and confessors who defend the hope in Christ against persecutors, but also those who introduce the power of the age to come into present-day history through their discipleship and spirituality, resisting evil powers, running risks and facing death daily (cf. 1 Cor. 15:31).

The supreme power of prayer

In transmitting the tradition of the Lord's supper St Paul clearly intended to describe an act in which the present community is made contemporary with Christ, who will not leave his disciples. The eucharist is not the only moment when such contemporaneity is realized in a sacramental manner; but this is a point in time when the intervention of God is, so to speak, guaranteed.

In the eucharist, the same Spirit who transforms the believer witnessing to truth before the powers into a "martyr" changes the "order of creation" (bread and wine) into the "order of grace". Only in and through the power of the Holy Spirit, and not as a result of a mechanical or magical action of the priest, is the sacramental action in the liturgy effective. The celebrant, says Cabasilas, brings "nothing of his own...; he offers only that which he has already received, whether it be matter, word or action, back to God".[18]

After the priest says the words of initiation, he confidently invokes the Holy Spirit: "We pray, we beseech and implore thee: Send down thy Holy Spirit upon us and upon these gifts here set forth."

> It is absolutely essential that those who make prayer should rely on God alone. For man could not even have imagined these things if God had not taught him of them: he could not have conceived the desire for them if God had not exhorted him; he could not have expected to receive it if he had not received the hope of it from him who is the Truth... As a result, the prayer is neither uncertain nor the result unsure... The sanctification of the mysteries is in the prayer of the priest, certainly not relying on any human power, but on the power of God.[19]

Here the "economy" of the Son and the "economy" of the Holy Spirit interpenetrate. Jesus Christ would not have commanded his apostles to "do this in remembrance of me" if he were not going to give them the power to do so.

> What then is this power? It is the Holy Spirit, the power from on high which has strengthened the apostles... Once come down, the Holy Spirit did not then forsake us, but he is with us, and he will remain until the end. It is for this purpose that the Saviour sent him...

But the Lord was not satisfied with sending the Holy Spirit to abide with us; he has himself promised to be with us, even unto the end of the world [Matt. 28:20]. The Paraclete is present unseen because he has not taken a human form, but by means of the great and holy mysteries the Lord submits himself to our sight and touch through the dread and holy mysteries, because he has taken our nature upon him and bears it eternally.[20]

The liturgy therefore offers a place where the action of the Holy Spirit is guaranteed and effective.

"Substantial bread"

The liturgy is an invitation not only to join the *ecclesia* but to share the daily food, the "substantial bread" which sustains the *ecclesia* in its pilgrimage of sanctification. The liturgy liberates the people to struggle for human holiness by partaking of the mysteries of Christ. Without the communion of the faithful, in which they receive provisions for the way of eternal life, the liturgy misses its purpose:

> No one has been "worthy" to receive communion, no one has been *prepared* for it. At this point all merits, all righteousness, all devotions disappear and dissolve. Life comes again to us as *gift*, a free and divine gift. This is why in the Orthodox church we call the eucharistic elements holy gifts. Adam is again introduced into Paradise, taken out of nothingness and crowned king of creation. Everything is free, nothing is due and yet all is given. And therefore the greatest humility and obedience is to *accept* the gift, to say yes — in joy and gratitude. There is nothing we can *do*, yet we become all that God wanted us to be from eternity, when we are *eucharistic*.[21]

Facing the world

Eucharist signals the centrality of Christ for the whole of creation and for all of humanity (cf. 2 Cor. 4:7; Matt. 28:18). Far from narrowing the Christocentric character of the New Testament by limiting Christ's dominion to the worshipping Christian community, the liturgy shows us Christ, the Lord of creation and history, repossessing heaven and earth (cf. Ps. 89:11):

> We... make petitions in charity for others, not only for the church and the rulers of the empire and those in danger and trouble and adversity, but indeed for all mankind throughout the world... Christians know that their God is common Lord of all, and that all things are in his care, since he made them, and if any man concerns himself with their welfare he honours God more than if he had offered him sacrifice [Matt. 9:13; 12:7; Hosea 6:6].

And then... we pray... that we ourselves, surrounded by peace, "may lead a quiet and peaceable life in all godliness and honesty" [1 Tim. 2:2]. And we do not ask only for the things of the spirit, but also for those material benefits which we require, for healthful air and an abundance of the fruits of the earth, in order that we may recognize God as Creator and Provider of all things and may look always to him; for Christ himself commanded us to ask of God even our daily bread, as well as all the other things.[22]

Each celebration of the liturgy actualizes what the crucified and risen Christ did in obedience to his Father for the whole creation and all of humanity. It is also the venue where the people of God receive the blessing of seeing the horizons of the kingdom. Eucharist anticipates God's invitation to this feast (cf. Luke 14:13). The liturgy begins and ends with the invocation of the kingdom. Here and now, on earth and in time, the liturgy inaugurates the eschatological community of the redeemed. As such it is also a moment of judgment for the Christian community — of how the kingdom of heaven is or is not present in the church as a sociological community, of how the church is or is not overcoming barriers to justice, freedom and solidarity, of how it is or is not an effective sign of something greater than the liturgical assembly.

The burning bush

In the liturgy believers participate in the act of prayer, celebration and sanctification "with our whole soul and with our whole mind", "unto hallowing of soul and body". Both flesh and spirit are involved. The icons require visual and pictorial sensitivity to inspire the imagination and contemplation. The processions put into motion the members of the body as if in a sacred dream. The great number of biblical words are used for personal communication away from the agitation of the world outside. The whole liturgy is a *dialogue*, an exchange of idioms and echoes, a combination of arts which reveal the mystery although it remains unknown. After each *kyrie eleison* there is a moment of silence when new feelings, "religious" feelings, are recovered, bringing inner stability and peace.

The participation of body and soul in the liturgy is not only a matter of psychology and ethics. It is related to Christ's holy humanity. We are partakers in the same process: his life-giving resurrection with his soul and body is given in the life-giving mysteries, in order to heal soul and body. His ascension is the ascension of humanity: "O Lord, whose glorious ascension made human flesh divine." We share the blessings of Pentecost by transforming our bodies into vessels and receptacles of the same Spirit.

Eucharist is received as the "fiery coal" which gives health and eternal life to soul and body: "I am refreshed and not consumed, even as the burning bush was not consumed."

NOTES

1. On the origin and development of the *ordo* of the liturgy see Alexander Schmemann, *Introduction to Liturgical Theology*, Crestwood NY, St Vladimir's Seminary Press, 1975.

2. Cf. *The Orthodox Liturgy*, London, Oxford UP, 1982; Alkiviadis Calivas, "Reflection on the Divine Liturgy", in *The Divine Liturgy*, Brookline MA, Holy Cross Orthodox Press, 1983, p.xiii.

3. Cf. Paul Meyendorff, "Liturgy", in N. Lossky et al., eds, *Dictionary of the Ecumenical Movement*, Geneva, WCC, 1991, pp.623-26.

4. For more detailed treatment, see Nicholas Cabasilas, *A Commentary on the Divine Liturgy*, tr. J.M. Hussey and P.A. McNulty, intro. R.M. French, London, SPCK, 1960. Cabasilas was a 14th-century Byzantine theologian; and his commentary in 53 chapters on the liturgy first appeared in Paris in 1560.

5. Cabasilas, *op. cit.*, pp.33f.

6. *Ibid.*, pp.75f.

7. *Ibid.*, pp.90f.

8. Cf. Ion Bria, *The Sense of Ecumenical Tradition*, Geneva, WCC, 1991, pp.49-59.

9. Cabasilas, *op. cit.*, p.84.

10. *Ibid.*, pp.88f.

11. *Ibid.*, pp.49f.

12. It may be noted in this connection that the theme of the seventh assembly of the World Council of Churches (Canberra 1991), "Come, Holy Spirit — Renew the Whole Creation", stimulated reflection on the person and action of the Holy Spirit in a trinitarian perspective, just as the theme of the previous assembly (Vancouver 1983), "Jesus Christ — the Life of the World", was placed in the same vision. As a result, a closer look was taken at how the image of the Trinity may influence the search for unity.

18   *The Liturgy after the Liturgy*

13. Cf. *Unseen Warfare*, Crestwood NY, St Vladimir's Seminary Press, 1978, p.183.

14. Two helpful explanations of this (in Romanian) are offered by Dumitru Staniloae, *Spirituality and Communion in the Orthodox Liturgy*, Craiova, Metropolia Oltenia Press, 1986; and Bishop Serafim, "Divine Liturgy", in *Orthodox Faith and Christian Life*, Sibiu, Metropolia Transylvania Press, 1992, pp.281-98.

15. Cabasilas, *op. cit.*, p.110.

16. In his commentary on the liturgy Cabasilas notes that both the Old and New Testaments record cases of God's spurning an offering because of a person's wickedness. However, he notes, "the holy gifts are offered twice; the first offering is made by the faithful, who place their gifts in the hands of the priests; the second is made by the church to God. If the offerer is in a state of serious sin, then his offering (the first of which we spoke) is of no avail, and brings him no benefit, because of his guilt... As for the second offering, if it is made by virtuous men, for the glory of God and his saints, and the salvation of the world, and every right intention in general, there is nothing to prevent it from being accepted. For the gifts have not been stained by the hands of him who first offered them; they have remained pure, they are consecrated and bring sanctification to those who approach them"; *ibid.*, pp.102f.

17. *Ibid.*, pp.88f.

18. *Ibid.*, p.104.

19. *Ibid.*, p.68.

20. *Ibid.*, pp.70f.

21. Alexander Schmemann, *For the Life of the World*, Crestwood NY, St Vladimir's Seminary Press, 1973, p.45.

22. Cabasilas, *op. cit.*, pp.46f.

2. The Liturgy after the Liturgy

Liturgy as witness ("martyria")

The idea of the "liturgy after the liturgy" emerged in the mid-1970s in ecumenical discussions of how the theology of mission (missiology) and the theology of the church (ecclesiology) are related. A key insight came from a consultation of Orthodox member churches of the World Council of Churches in Bucharest in June 1974, convened to prepare a working paper on "Confessing Christ Today" for the WCC's fifth assembly (Nairobi 1975):

> If Christ's mission brings about essentially nothing less than the self-giving of God's trinitarian life to the world, it follows that mission is ultimately possible only in and through *an event of communion which reflects in history the trinitarian existence of God himself.* The church is meant precisely to be that. Mission, therefore, suffers and is seriously distorted or disappears whenever it is not possible to point to a community in history which reflects this trinitarian existence of communion. This happens whenever the church is so distorted or divided that it is no longer possible to recognize it as such a communion, or whenever mission is exercised without reference to the church, but with reference simply to the individuals or the social realities of history.[1]

In other words, ecclesiological heresy may make mission impossible.

This was further developed at a consultation in Etchmiadzin, Armenia, in 1975, on "Confessing Christ through the Liturgical Life of the Church Today". Its report noted that the eucharistic liturgy has implications not only for the being and identity of the church but also for its mission in the world:

> The risen Christ is made manifest and present by the Holy Spirit in the liturgical life, through word and sacraments. The whole life and prayer of the church's members, whether meeting together for common worship or celebrating each one "in the temple of the heart", centres on the eucharist. Here all the prayers and liturgical acts of the people of God converge; here the church discovers its true identity. In the whole field of Christian spirituality, eucharistic spirituality creates a dynamic piety, mystical bonds with Christ, which overcome evil by living fully the mystery of incarnation and divinization in all its dimensions...
>
> In the liturgical celebration, extending into the daily life of the church's members, the church announces and achieves the advent of the kingdom of the holy Trinity. In all things it commemorates the glorified Christ and gives

thanks to God in Jesus Christ. The entire tradition of the church, its worship, its theology and its preaching, is a doxology, a continual thanksgiving, a confession of faith in Christ's Easter triumph and man's liberation from all the forces which oppress and degrade him. Prayer and the eucharist, whereby Christians overcome their selfish ways, impel them also to become involved in the social and political life of their respective countries.[2]

Out of this idea of the extension of the liturgical celebration into the daily life of the faithful in the world came the concept of the "liturgy after the liturgy".[3] The dynamics of the liturgy go beyond the boundaries of the eucharistic assembly to serve the community at large. The eucharistic liturgy is not an escape into an inner realm of prayer, a pious turning away from social realities; rather, it calls and sends the faithful to celebrate "the sacrament of the brother" outside the temple in the public marketplace, where the cries of the poor and marginalized are heard.

Anastasios Yannoulatos, then a professor at the University of Athens, underscored the necessary link between taking part "in the great event of liberation from sin and of communion with Christ" and making evident "this transfiguration of our little being into a member of Christ" in daily life:

> Each of the faithful is called upon to continue a personal "liturgy" on the secret altar of his own heart, to realize a living proclamation of the good news "for the sake of the whole world". Without this continuation the liturgy remains incomplete... The sacrifice of the eucharist must be extended in personal sacrifices for the people in need, the brothers for whom Christ died... The continuation of liturgy in life means a continuous liberation from the powers of the evil that are working inside us, a continual reorientation and openness to insights and efforts aimed at liberating human persons from all demonic structures of injustice, exploitation, agony, loneliness, and at creating real communion of persons in love.[4]

Anastasios describes this everyday personal attitude as "liturgical" because (1) it is energized by participation in the eucharist; (2) it constitutes the best preparation for a more conscious participation in the eucharist; and (3) it is a clear and living expression of the real transformation of men and women in Christ.

The typology of "liturgy after the liturgy" is also reflected in the reports of the WCC's 1980 conference on world mission and evangelism in Melbourne, which spoke of the eucharist as "pilgrim bread", emphasized the role of worship in educating and nurturing the "martyrs" of the church, those who witness to Christ's resurrection in the world, and recognized the evangelizing force of the very act of coming together for eucharist in certain circumstances:

> We hear of those who come together at great risk, and whose courage reveals to those around them how precious is this sacrament. In other situations the eucharist may be an open-air witness so planned that many may see it. Such a joyful celebration as this may offer fresh hope in cynical, secular societies. There is, at the Lord's table, a vision of God which draws the human heart to the Lord.[5]

The urgent need to recover the unity between worship and daily Christian life was summarized by the WCC's sixth assembly (Vancouver 1983) as follows:

> For the sake of the witnessing vocation of the church we need to find a true rhythm of Christian involvement in the world. The church is gathered for worship and scattered for everyday life. While in some situations in the witnessing dimension of worship there must be a "liturgy after the liturgy",... it must be stressed that there is no Christian service to the world unless it is rooted in the service of worship.[6]

The significance of worship as a means for evangelism was also emphasized by the seventh assembly (Canberra 1991):

> The fundamental nature of the Christian life is to gather around word and sacrament in fellowship and prayer (Acts 2:42). The experience of worship is both the stimulus for and the result of the inner relationship with the Spirit. It involves life, gives life, and is a means for evangelism and grassroots ecumenism. Every worshipping community should be a model for an inclusive community. Worship space needs to be designed so that all people are able to participate fully. A lively ministry of hospitality, welcoming all in the name of the Lord, is most important. The plea of young people for forms of worship and celebration which fit their culture must be taken seriously.[7]

In ensuing ecumenical discussions other dimensions of "the liturgy after the liturgy" have been discovered.[8] The church's liturgical and diaconal functions are connected, for liturgy reshapes the social life of Christians with a new emphasis on the sharing of bread, on the healing of brokenness, on reconciliation and on justice in the human community.[9] The concept has also come to be associated with a other facets of the life of the church, including education,[10] evangelization, [11] concern for creation, [12] spirituality[13] and social ethics.[14] The church's WCC's Vancouver assembly spoke about the "eucharistic vision of ecumenism".[15]

Perhaps a major reason for the ecumenical importance attached to the liturgy after the liturgy in the 1970s and 1980s is that, under the burden of despotic and totalitarian regimes, the *Kyrie eleison* of the modest and sometimes hidden Sunday liturgy was the only collective cry for truth, love and mercy.[16] The ecumenical community learned a good deal from the resistance of the Orthodox churches under communist regimes and Soviet domination, through the network of popular communities who never ceased to believe in the force of the eucharistic liturgy:

> Sometimes historical circumstances will demand that the Christian witness to the God of Jesus Christ take the form of a *martyria* in the strongest sense of the term... The history of the church affords many examples to show that God's grace will not fail his elect, even in the extremity of their suffering. Often it has been very explicitly from the eucharist that Christians under trial have drawn the divine strength which gives them courage and keeps them faithful... Already at the beginning of the second century, St Ignatius of Antioch foresees that his martyrdom will "grind" him into one bread with Christ. Fifty years later, the martyr Polycarp will give to his parting prayer the form of a *eucharistia*.
>
> Especially in difficult circumstances, the very celebration of the eucharist can constitute an act of witness. In "impossible" situations, it proclaims that God alone creates a saving future. When it cries "Maranatha", the eucharistic community is calling for the overthrow of all that is opposed to God; it is praying for the final coming of God's kingdom "Let grace come: let this world pass away" (*Didache*, 10). This hoped-for future is already prefigured in the fact that the eucharistic community itself includes pardoned sinners, reconciled adversaries and the desperate restored to life: all are welcomed by the Lord at his table of justice, peace and joy in the Holy Spirit (cf. Rom. 14:17).[17]

Important contributions to the evolution of this concept were also made by the "eucharistic ecclesiology" elaborated by Orthodox theologians in Britain, France and the USA, as well as from the experience of emerging churches in Africa and Asia.[18]

Essential connections

The liturgy is constituted by pairing certain realities which cannot thereafter be disconnected. Too often, however, one-sided interpretations put the life of the churches in contradiction with the liturgy:

> The meaning of the liturgy has been often obscured by one-sided interpretations, in which it was presented almost exclusively as a means of

individual sanctification. It is urgent, therefore, that we rediscover the initial *lex orandi* of the church in its cosmic, redemptive and *eschatological* dimensions. Behind this static and individualistic understanding of the liturgy we must recover its dynamic nature and power. It edifies and fulfils the church as the sacrament of the kingdom; it transforms us, the members of the church, into the *witnesses* of Christ and his co-workers.[19]

One evidence that liturgical practice and ritual have become disconnected from authentic Orthodox ecclesiology is the decreased involvement of the people in the liturgy and communion.[20] Moreover, despite the courageous celebration of the liturgy under communist regimes to which we referred above, ignorance of the Bible and the tradition have become more and more pronounced in these countries. The tradition is not only a treasure that needs to be preserved but also something that must live in the process of being transmitted.

This raises the difficult problem of the language of the liturgy. One of the blatant contradictions in the Orthodox churches is the celebration of the liturgy in ancient languages which are no longer spoken or written by the people. While these liturgical languages should not be allowed to disappear, because of their important impact on culture as a whole and the identity of the church, room should also be made for the introduction of the vernacular into the liturgy. Young people must also be prepared to follow the services with understanding. If the language and vocabulary make the text impossible to understand, the people are bound to ignore it. This inevitably breaks any connection between the liturgy and the liturgy after the liturgy.[21]

But there is a further problem. Under the guise of avoiding the temptation of "horizontalizing" the Christian message or subjecting it to "social" and "political" concerns, the Orthodox have often proposed a way of life which cannot be translated into action in society. They place the social order and secular issues into the hands of the state and the political parties. Hence they are unable to translate their theological vision into the terms of the prevailing intellectual and political culture. They have ignored the social and political consequences of *theosis* (deification) and disregarded the historical concretization of eucharistic spirituality.[22] In so doing they interrupt the flow of the liturgical act, breaking off diakonia at the end of worship, at the door of the church.[23]

Basileia, the rule of God, is the centre of the liturgy: "Blessed is the kingdom of the Father, and of the Son, and of the Holy Spirit." Preaching the good news of the *basileia* of God means challenging the unjust and totalitarian structures of society. The liturgy is not just the telling of the story of Jesus Christ, but the interpretation and concretization of his death on the cross and his resurrection. Because the *basileia* is invoked, Christian witness as struggle and confrontation must never be allowed to disappear from the horizon of the liturgy.[24]

The basic structure of the liturgy is based on two movements: first the people gather for worship, to hear the word of God and to eat the bread of life (cf. Luke 4:16); then, at the end of the liturgy, they are sent out (cf. Matt. 28:19f.). Here the worshipping community becomes an evangelizing community. Receiving the eucharistic "bread for pilgrims", food for missionaries, the faithful become actors of mission. The liturgical assembly is transformed into a "cloud of witnesses", together with all saints, confessors and martyrs. The church sends its members on the way of the apostles, knowing what Jesus told them: "Whoever does not gather with me scatters" (Matt. 12:30). The church grows by adding new members to the original apostolic community founded on the day of Pentecost in Jerusalem, where the disciples experienced historically the fulfilment of Jesus' prayer "that all may be one" (John 17:23).

This one universal church is not an abstract entity; it is found historically in particular places and times. This points to a second essential connection: the pairing of the liturgy and indigenous culture. The liturgy is a clue to understanding the polyphony of the local churches united in their episcopal conciliarity and cultural diversity. The bishop as celebrant of the eucharist is at one and the same time the symbol of apostolic fidelity, local unity and universal communion or catholicity.

> Eucharistic ecclesiology focuses on the miracle of the unity of the early Christian church, which really existed only in the local churches without yet being bound together by councils and general structures of church government; yet everywhere this early Christian church was the one, holy, catholic and apostolic church. Where by the operation of the Holy Spirit the Lord is sacramentally present in his world and his reconciling sacrificial death, and the congregation is gathered around him in praise and worship, there the church in all its plenitude is present. For St Ignatius of Antioch, its unity was visible in the one president of the eucharistic assembly, the bishop and the successor of the apostles; the multiplicity of interrelated ministries expressed the richness of the divine love in the mystery of the holy Trinity, as the church fathers testify.[25]

"Local church" refers primarily to the incarnation of the universal among a particular people through its own culture and language. The *church of nations* is at the heart of the whole history of Orthodox mission. It is important for the local church to manifest its cultural identity, but this must not be confused with nationalism. The local church is not an invention of national states — although it can become a national institution — but is the fruit of proclaiming the gospel through the liturgy to a particular people. In some parts of the Orthodox world the anomaly remains that indigenous people do not yet have full cultural autonomy (Greek is used in Palestinian lands) or canonical autocephaly (there are non-indigenous leaders of Orthodox churches in Jerusalem, Africa, Asia and Latin America). Meanwhile, aspirations for autonomy and autocephaly within Orthodox churches in newly independent countries in Europe have created sharp tensions within the worldwide Orthodox family.

At the koinonia around the holy table in the liturgy, there is a vision of God inviting all humanity to participate in his precious celestial gifts. Here is another essential connection: the sharing of one bread and one cup together within the church must have its counterpart in the life of the community. As we share the same eucharistic bread, we must also share our food and existence with our neighbours. St John Chrysostom spoke about the liturgy which takes place outside the temple, where the altar raised by the poor people must be reinstated by the Christians. It is the "sacrament of the brother", the brothers of Christ, the poor.

This logic of serving at the brother's altar has motivated the church to develop a witness in society, but the church can easily bypass this requirement of the liturgy by what it says or fails to say during the liturgy. The church can be diverted by social and political considerations, especially by the lust for power and hegemony, which contradict the liturgical values of sacrifice, reconciliation, justice and sharing. The liturgy has a mechanism which rejects the distance between ecclesiastical hierarchy and the people, between a clerical church and the body of the faithful. The institutional church must thus remain transparent and flexible if it is to be an instrument in the hands of the faithful for effective Christian action.

The political culture of the Eastern tradition has been determined by the choice of Christianity as the official religion of the empire following the conversion of Constantine in the fourth century. Later, the theory of a *symphony* between state and church, patriarch and empire, became part of the political doctrine of the church. While the Constantinian era as a political reality has been over since 1917, many Orthodox retain their nostalgia for the protection of the empire. Even after the tragic experience of state-church relationships under the communists, the topic of separating church and state remains a taboo subject. But the spirit of the liturgy does not allow the suppression of hidden realities and moral heresies. It is important to know how far Christian values and moral convictions have been compromised by the "symphony". The liturgy inevitably raises the issue of ecclesiology and ethics; it is inevitably concerned with the destructive nature of political powers. In such cases it can inspire dissidence and civil disobedience.

The Orthodox churches' anchoring of tradition in a certain period of history, the period of the "ancient undivided churches" and the great ecumenical councils, brings with it a sense of conciliarity which recognizes the polyphony of the local churches and the doctrinal symbol of common tradition. The liturgy also reflects this broad conciliar spirit. Before holy communion the believer must personally confess the creed, repeating the baptismal confession, "I believe in one God..." Does this model of eucharistic catholicity provide sufficient ground for comprehensive reception of various Christian churches at the Lord's table? Is the liturgical "economy" not a way to restore broken communion?

The rediscovery of this *ecclesiology of communion* is at the centre of the typology of the "liturgy after the liturgy". Stimulated to clarify their missiology ecumenically, the Orthodox felt the need also to renew their ecclesiology, to recapture lost or forgotten dimensions of the doctrine of the church, the witnessing people of God in the world created by God. The essential connection must be maintained between ecclesiology and missiology, between the proclamation of *basileia* and the building up of the body of Christ in history as sacrament of the kingdom.

The ecclesiology of communion or koinonia is a critical principle for understanding the nature and mission of the church, offering several significant clarifications:
— correction of an ecclesiology informed by the Constantinian ideology of Christendom. The church is not a Christian institution of the empire, but the *ecclesia* of the scattered people in all nations;
— rediscovery of God's "economy" for the whole *oikoumene*; hence, God's preferential option for the poor;
— creation of concern about poverty, marginalization and suffering, because koinonia is the opposite of exclusion;
— an understanding of tradition not only as fidelity to the experience of the early church but also as an instrument of renewal and a movement for mission; a recognition, therefore, that worship needs new symbols to capture something of the mystery of God in contemporary society;

— emphasis on the need to confront the problem of how to communicate, including the issue of the hearer, of the message itself and of identity through the ages.

The dynamics of liturgy in mission

It is a false, but unfortunately common stereotype among Christians of other traditions that the Orthodox churches are "non-missionary" churches. On this view, they are preoccupied with their doctrinal and ritual integrity, enclosed within their national frontiers and indifferent to the proclamation of the gospel, the conversion of the nations or the growth in the number of Christians in the world. The growth of proselytism in the areas of Orthodox churches, especially in Central and Eastern Europe since the fall of communism, attests to the fact that their way of evangelization is unknown or disregarded as completely inadequate. While the missionary and social failures of the Orthodox churches over many centuries cannot be overlooked, it is not correct to say that they have abandoned their responsibility for apostolic ministry and diakonia. The Orthodox have chosen their way of understanding and undertaking mission. As they celebrate the liturgy, they are equipping, nourishing and sending missionaries outside. Tradition is also true mission, because it implies a creative encounter between gospel and culture.

It is important to recognize this in ecumenical missiology, which should foster a continuous process of mutual correction among the many diverse missionary traditions, methodologies and strategies. In the words of the WCC's 1980 world mission conference in Melbourne:

> We are aware of different emphases, but believe there is a growing ecumenical consensus... We would seek to value the spoken word as having a sacramental quality, for in preaching we ask the Spirit to take our crude words and thoughts and make them effective and loving to touch the hearts of our hearers. We would seek to receive the eucharist as God's word which speaks freshly each day of sacrifice and victory. We believe that as our churches hold together these two aspects of Christian sharing, we may avoid both the excessive intellectualism of some preaching traditions and the excessive ritualism of some who have focused entirely on the eucharist.[26]

The evangelizing and witnessing potentialities of the eucharistic liturgy extend to other kinds of liturgies and forms of diakonia outside the walls of the church. What is at stake here is the continuous building up of the church, the body of Christ, the sacrament of the kingdom of God in history. To strengthen the diaconal role of the worshipping community scattered for daily life, this second movement of the liturgy, the eucharist has to become "pilgrim bread", food for missionaries, nourishment for Christians involved in social and moral struggles.

By contrast, there are many churches today in which few people even receive holy communion as an integral part of the liturgy. Many people are not committed to mission and evangelism because they do not understand the liturgical language, the depth and meaning of the rites, especially during the first part of the liturgy of the word, which is the missionary section par excellence. An extreme abstraction and a lack of contact with human reality and the physical universe are entirely contrary to the spirit of the liturgy.

In the eucharist the church community enjoys a moment of affirmation of the reality of being in Christ. It is the icon of Christ; it is the cosmos becoming *ecclesia*. The people touch the mystery; they have a foretaste of the kingdom with all their physical senses — listening to the prayers and the music, seeing the icons and the processions of the gospel and the gifts, eating and drinking the Lord's supper. Above all, the eucharistic liturgy is not terminated in the prayerful intimacy of the worship, but it continues with diakonia, apostolic mission, visible and public Christian witness.

But the liturgy is not simply a tool for confessing Christ or an instrument of mission; rather, it must be seen as the starting event of the Christian movement for mission, the point of departure given to the church for pursuing its vocation in the wider society, which is also a point of arrival.

The significance of the eucharist for the communion of the faithful, the renewal and sanctification of creation, the missionary witness of Christ is strongly underscored by the *Baptism, Eucharist and Ministry* document:

> The eucharist embraces all aspects of life. It is a representative act of thanksgiving and offering on behalf of the whole world. The eucharistic celebration demands reconciliation and sharing among all those regarded as brothers and sisters in the one family of God and is a constant challenge in the search for appropriate relationship in social, economic and political life... All kinds of injustice, racism, separation and lack of freedom are radically challenged when we share in the body and blood of Christ. Through the eucharist the all-renewing grace of God penetrates and restores human personality and dignity. The eucharist involves the believer in the central event of the world's history. As participants in the eucharist, therefore, we prove inconsistent if we are not actively participating in this ongoing restoration of the world's situation and the human condition...

Solidarity in the eucharistic communion of the body of Christ and responsible care of Christians for one another and the world find specific expression in the liturgies: in the mutual forgiveness of sins; the sign of peace; intercession for all; the eating and drinking together; the taking of the elements to the sick and those in prison or the celebration of eucharist with them. All these manifestations of love in the eucharist are directly related to Christ's own testimony as a servant, in whose servanthood Christians themselves participate...

Reconciled in the eucharist, the members of the body of Christ are called to be servants of reconciliation among men and women and witnesses of the joy of resurrection. As Jesus went out to publicans and sinners and had table-fellowship with them during his earthly ministry, so Christians are called in the eucharist to be in solidarity with the outcast and to become signs of the love of Christ who lived and sacrificed himself for all and now gives himself in the eucharist.[27]

All this inevitably raises the issues of concelebration and eucharistic communion with churches which have different ecclesiological views on the liturgy. "Liturgy after the liturgy" stands for the catholicity of the eucharist. It is the priest's responsibility to encourage all people who take part in the offertory and the *anaphora* to come for holy communion. At his discretion he may give communion to members of Oriental Orthodox, Roman Catholic and Old Catholic churches without formal conversion to the Orthodox church.

Of course, the way for full eucharistic communion needs solid preparation. For the Orthodox this will mean re-examining their deeply entrenched evasive attitude regarding the history and vocation of those Christians who do not belong to their own church. It is important to conceive all churches in the framework of an ecumenical conciliarity and from the perspective of the catholicity of the eucharist, no longer taking for granted that the particular traditions of other churches have merely secondary authority. To blame other Christians for being Catholics or Protestants or Evangelicals, to describe them as "heterodox" and treat them as strangers, will only deepen the wounds of separation. All Christians ought to feel settled and joyful with their origin and church affiliation and together with other Christians as pilgrims on the way to fuller koinonia.

At the same time, we must clearly identify the concrete points of separation which continue to constitute a defeat for all the churches. Ecumenism challenges our sinful clinging to sectarianism and integrism. We have to rediscover such ecumenical resources as the litany for unity which is a part of many Christian liturgies, for as long as there is a prayer "for peace in the whole world, for the stability of the holy churches of God and for the unity of all" there is hope for unity in koinonia.

Most contemporary missionary methods, which continue those which evolved between the 16th and 19th centuries, reflect the attachment of Protestants to biblical texts and sermons or of Roman Catholics to ecclesiastical institutions and sacraments. One lesson that could be drawn from Orthodox history is the dynamic of the eucharistic assembly for the proclamation of the gospel, the sharing of the bread of life with others and the visible communion of the people. This way of evangelizing remains largely ignored, which, as we said earlier, explains in part at least the growth of proselytism in Orthodox countries.[28]

From the beginning, the celebration of the Lord's supper at a particular time (Sunday, the day of Christ's resurrection) and in a particular holy place was at the heart of the Christian community (*ecclesia*). Borrowing some of the rituals used in the synagogues and temple of apostolic times, but based on the words of Jesus Christ, the liturgy was meant to transform the worshippers and send them on an apostolic journey into the *oikoumene*: "Their voice has gone out to all the earth, and their words to the ends of the world" (Rom. 10:18).

The liturgy goes beyond the appropriation of Christ's message of salvation to transform Christians into witnesses to the risen Christ. The joy of sharing the very life of Christ, in the form of the eucharistic bread and wine, should be transmitted to others. Through the liturgy of the word — biblical readings, homily, litanies and responses — the faithful are learning a language of communication in order to reach other people who are looking for faith. The eucharist itself is given as "pilgrim bread", as nourishment for exhausted pilgrims, sometimes martyrs of the cross. This is why, at the end of the liturgy, the priests bless their apostolic journey — "Go forth in peace" — in order to give an account of the Christian faith, hope and love.

The liturgy reminds us that the church is built on the foundations of the apostles, the cornerstone being Jesus Christ himself (in fact, the altar-stone stands for Christ). The images of the apostles, which are visible in the church in various forms, symbolize the multitude of nations who will be converted to Christ, joining the Jerusalem community, for historically the apostles went into all parts of the world to preach the gospel and establish local churches:

The church is planted in the world for the healing of the nations. The church should not be seen simply as a Noah's Ark to salvage a few specimens of the human race about to perish. The Holy Spirit came upon that small Jerusalem community on the day of Pentecost in order that, through them and through others who were to believe in Christ through their word (John 17:20), the world may be healed and redeemed.[29]

The church is a holy place because it symbolizes the venue of the coming of the kingdom of God. It is essential to challenge individualistic approaches to mission with the reminder that Christ formed those who believed in him into his body, the church, the sign and sacrament of the kingdom.

In the Orthodox tradition, there is no private or isolated liturgy. Since all are celebrating the same faith, all are at the same time concelebrants and communicants: praying, singing, chanting, confessing their faith. The liturgical community gathered together "to do this in remembrance of me" is by this very fact a witnessing community. As a place of gathering for praying and sharing the body and blood of Christ, every local parish is also a point of departure into the world to share the joy of resurrection. The worshipping assembly is prepared and sent as an evangelizing community. Therefore, for the Orthodox, the missionary life and structure of every parish is the key to practising the proclamation of Christ today. For the responsibility of every believer does not end at the geographical and cultural borders of the community in which he or she lives, but extends to other communities, including the people who do not know the gospel.

In the liturgy the verbal proclamation of the gospel is inseparable from the doxological way of praying and symbolic ritual of the sacraments. This prevents the Orthodox from separating doctrine and prayer, biblical texts from hymnology, biblical stories from the life of saints. It overcomes the contradiction between doctrinal teachings and personal experiences. *Lex credendi* goes together with *lex orandi*.

Liturgy opens the horizon of the kingdom of God for all humanity in the midst of history. It opens the communion of God for scattered people. There is a sacred time and a sacred place where people bring forth everything of their own existence and commit their lives into the hands of the Creator and Saviour: "Thine own, of thine own, we offer unto thee in all and for all."

Orthodox theologian K.M. George draws a contrast between the "saint" in the Orthodox tradition and the "crusading missionary":

The saint prays and receives the creation of God with hospitality. The missionary preaches and offers, often aggressively, in order to give... The world, however, is healed and transfigured more by the praying saint than by the thundering preachers. It is the saint who, manifesting God's tender love and receiving all creatures in divine hospitality, is genuinely sensitive to the riches of other religions, to different cultures, to "all sentient beings". The crusading missionary is afire with the message he proclaims, but can be totally lacking in receptivity and sensitivity... Today we need to combine in our experience of our church the true saint and the genuine missionary whose sole concern is manifesting the kingdom and not annexing new territories.[30]

The church grows by increasing the Pentecost community, by bringing new members into Christ's body: "I have other sheep that do not belong to this fold. I must bring them also, and they will listen to my voice. So there will be one flock, one shepherd" (John 10:16). On the cross he assumes the sufferings of all. He incorporates into the people of God those who were excluded (Luke 5:27-32; 19:1-10), offering koinonia to all scattered. By celebrating baptism and eucharist, the church opens the koinonia of God to everyone, becoming a fellowship of all nations.

NOTES

1. From the report of the consultation in *International Review of Mission*, Vol. 64, no. 253, 1975, p.79.

2. For the text, see Georges Tsetsis, ed., *Orthodox Thought*, Geneva, WCC, 1983, pp.6f. See also *International Review of Mission*, Vol. 64, no. 256, 1975, pp.417-21; I. Bria, ed., *Martyria-Mission: The Witness of the Orthodox Churches Today*, Geneva, WCC, 1980, pp.231-34.

3. Cf. Ion Bria, "The 'liturgy' after the liturgy", *International Review of Mission*, Vol. 67, no. 265, 1978, pp.86-90; reprinted in *Go Forth in Peace: A Pastoral and Missionary Guidebook*, Geneva, WCC, 1982, pp.28-41; and in G. Limouris, ed., *Orthodox Visions of Ecumenism*, Geneva, WCC, 1994, pp.216-20.

4. *Martyria-Mission*, p.67.

5. From the report of Section III, "The Church Witnesses to the Kingdom", para. 31a, in *Your Kingdom Come: Mission Perspectives*, Geneva, WCC, 1980, p.205. The social dimensions and missionary repercussions of the sacramental life of Orthodoxy were also discussed in the preparations for the 1989 conference on world mission and evangelism (San Antonio); cf. Georges Lemopoulos, ed., *Your Will Be Done: Orthodoxy in Mission*, Geneva, WCC, and Katerini, Tertios, 1989.

6. David Gill, ed., *Gathered for Life: Official Report of the WCC's Sixth Assembly*, Geneva, WCC, 1983, p.35.

7. Michael Kinnamon, ed., *Signs of the Spirit: Official Report of the WCC Seventh Assembly*, Geneva, WCC, 1991, p.119.

8. A consultation on "The Ecumenical Nature of Orthodox Witness" (New Valamo, Finland, 1977) was the first to speak of "the dynamics of the concept of 'liturgy after the liturgy'"; the text of the report is in Limouris, ed., *Orthodox Visions of Ecumenism*, pp.66-69.

9. Cf. Myra Blyth, "Liturgy after the Liturgy: An Ecumenical Perspective", *The Ecumenical Review*, Vol. 44, no. 1, 1992, pp.73-79.

10. Jan Anchimiuk, "Ministry of the Eucharistic Liturgy and the Ministry of the Liturgy after the Liturgy", in Tsetsis, ed., *Orthodox Thought*, pp.31f.

11. Cf. Aram Keshishian, *Orthodox Perspectives on Mission*, Oxford, Regnum-Lynx, 1992, pp.22-30.

12. Cf. Gennadios Limouris, "The Eucharist as Sacrament of Sharing", in *Orthodox Visions of Ecumenism*, p.253.

13. D. Ciobotea, "Spiritual Formation and Liturgical Life", in S. Amirtham and Robin Pryor, eds, *Resources for Spiritual Formation in Theological Education*, Geneva, WCC, 1989, pp.23-30.

14. Cf. E. Clapsis, "Ecclesiology and Ethics: Reflections by an Orthodox Theologian", *The Ecumenical Review*, Vol. 47, no. 2, 1995, pp.161-63; "The Eucharist as Missionary Event in a Suffering World", in *Your Will Be Done*, p.101.

15. *Gathered for Life*, p.45; cf. A. Keshishian, *Conciliar Fellowship: A Common Goal*, Geneva, WCC, 1992, pp.42ff.

16. Cf. Boris Bobrinskoy, "Prière du coeur et eucharistie", in *Person and Communion: Homage to Fr D. Staniloae*, Sibiu, 1993, p.631.

17. *Sharing in One Hope*, report of the meeting of the WCC commission on Faith and Order in Bangalore; Geneva, WCC, 1978, pp.197f.

18. Some of these themes are reviewed in greater detail in several of my articles, among them, "The Church's Role in Evangelism: Icon or Platform?", *International Review of Mission*, Vol. 64, 1975, pp.243-50; "Reflections on Mission Theology and Methodology", *ibid.*, Vol. 73, no. 289, 1984, pp.66-72; "Mission and Secularization in Europe", *ibid.*, Vol. 77, no. 305, 1988, pp.117-30; "Renewal in Mission", *ibid.*,

34 *The Liturgy after the Liturgy*

Vol. 80, no. 317, 1991, pp.55-59; "Diaspora, mission et ecclésiologie", *Service Orthodoxe de Presse* (Paris), no. 15, 1977, pp.8-10; "La signification missionaire de l'Eucharistie", *ibid.*, no. 62, 1981, pp.15-20; "Théologie de la mission", *ibid.*, no. 85, 1984, pp.17-24; "Eucharistie et évangelisation", *Lettre sur l'Evangelisation* (Geneva), nos 3-4, 1981, pp.2-6; "Unité des chrétiens et mission de l'Eglise", *Spiritus*, no. 88, 1982, pp.293-300; "Biserica si Liturghia", *Ortodoxia*, Vol. 34, No. 4, 1982, pp.481-91; "Ecclésiologie: Préoccupations et mutations actuelles", *Unité Chrétienne*, no. 70, 1983, pp.45-88; "Faith and Worship", *One World*, no. 141, 1988, pp.15f.

19. Report of a consultation on "Preaching and Teaching the Christian Faith Today" (Zica Monastery, Yugoslavia, 1980), in Tsetsis, ed., *Orthodox Thought*, pp.62f. On the link between worship, mission and culture, see also Anastasios Yannoulatos, "Thy Will Be Done: Mission in Christ's Way", in J.A. Scherer and Stephen B. Bevans, eds, *New Directions in Mission and Evangelization*, Maryknoll NY, Orbis, 1994, pp.26-38; John Meyendorff, "Christ as Word: Gospel and Culture", *International Review of Mission*, Vol. 74, no. 294, 1985, pp.32-43; Sava Christos Agouridis, "Evangelisation et monde moderne", in Agouridis and René Girault, eds, *Annoncer Jésus-Christ aujourd'hui*, Paris, Mame, 1973, pp.11-48; Geevarghese Mar Osthathios, "The Gospel of the Kingdom and the Crucified and Risen Lord", in *Your Kingdom Come*, pp.37-51; Paulos Mar Gregorios, *The Meaning and Nature of Diakonia*, Geneva, WCC, 1988.

20. Alexander Schmemann, *For the Life of the World*, Crestwood NY, St Vladimir's Seminary Press, 1973, p.45.

21. Cf. "Orthodox Mission in the 9th Century: The Witness of St Methodius", *International Review of Mission*, Vol. 74, no. 294, 1985, pp.217-18.

22. Cf. "Salvation in Orthodox Theology", report of a consultation in Greece, 1972, in *Orthodox Contributions to Nairobi*, Geneva, WCC, 1975, pp.7-10.

23. Cf. Ion Bria, "Ecclésiologie et sociologie", in *Le défi de l'Europe post-communiste et l'engagement social chrétien*, Fribourg, Editions Universitaires, 1994, pp.69-75.

24. Cf. Metropolitan John of Pergamon, "The Church as Communion", in *On the Way to Fuller Koinonia* (report of the fifth world conference on Faith and Order), Geneva, WCC, 1994, p.106.

25. Fairy von Lilienfeld, "'Visions of Europe' with Divided Churches?", in J.S. Pobee, ed., *Construction of a Common European Home*, Geneva, WCC, 1994, pp.87f.

26. *Your Kingdom Come*, pp.203f.

27. *Baptism, Eucharist and Ministry*, Geneva, WCC, 1982, p.14; the entire section (paras 19-26) from which these excerpts are taken is worth reading in this connection.

28. Cf. Raymond Fung, *Evangelistically Yours: Ecumenical Letters on Contemporary Evangelism*, Geneva, WCC, 1992, pp.92-126; Karel Blei, *On Being the Church Across Frontiers*, Geneva, WCC, 1992, pp.73-81.

29. *Jesus Christ — The Life of the World*, Geneva, WCC, 1982, p.6.

30. K.M. George, "Mission for Unity or Unity for Mission?", in *Your Will Be Done*, pp.158f.

3. Ecumenical Orientations in Liturgy

Certainly, liturgy implies and recognizes the structure of ecclesiology. The church is not an anonymous abstraction. But the very fact that the worshipping community is relational, both in receiving God's gifts and in sharing them with others, challenges an ecclesiology which turns around itself and is centred on ecclesiastical institutions. While the identity of the local church is given by the ministry of the bishop, who proclaims the gospel, teaches the faith and nurtures the people into an inclusive community in a given place, we must not lose sight of the purpose of the church served by this structure. Belonging to a community is a condition of being a Christian (1 John 2:19). Being in the church means "to share in the inheritance of the saints in the light" (Col. 1:12). In providing a context for proclamation, serving, feeding, the liturgy aims to lead the people into a life of communion, and the quality of this communion is essential for its mission.

It is important to remember that in the celebration of eucharist both parts of the church are present: "We represent in this mystery the cherubim". The communion of saints is also recalled: "Having remembered all the saints". Among the saints there is a special place for Mary, the mother of God: "Especially for our glorious lady Theotokos". An ecclesiology which does not include Mary the mother of Jesus is unbiblical. Equally, a feminist theology which does not consider her role, complementary to her son, is misplaced. Certainly, the debate about the role of women in the church, including the ordination of women to the priesthood and episcopate, will take on another perspective if we consider the complementary role of Mary within the apostolic church.

The criteria for apostolicity

The letter to the Hebrews summarizes the elements of apostolicity in the Christian community: "Remember your leaders, those who spoke the word of God to you, consider the outcome of their way of life, and imitate their faith" (Heb. 13:7). The liturgy reflects this apostolicity of the church in a variety of ways.

Proclamation and interpretation of the gospel. The community strongly affirms that the Word became flesh. Incarnation means that God, in order to redeem humanity, assumed the human form and condition. The liturgy of the word ends with a confession of sins, reminding the faithful that they are subject to the same human condition which Jesus appropriated.

Confession of the apostolic faith. The words of the Nicene-Constantinopolitan Creed (381) are a conciliar expression of the apostolic faith and remain a symbol of apostolic community.[1] In confessing it, the church is sure that it is not following "strange teachings" (Heb. 13:9). It is here that the unity of churches begins, in recognizing each other in the ecumenical creed as people of faith.

The visible local community. Celebration of the eucharist together with the communion of saints, is an anticipatory fulfilment of the kingdom. The celebrant, called to this action and ordained in the context of the eucharist, is the symbol of the historical relationship between the present community and the apostolic community. The eucharist which the faithful share through holy communion is the bread of the first Christians.

The experience of Christ outside the temple. As a community made contemporary with Christ, the liturgical assembly must witness in the world to the suffering and risen Christ. Christ's disciples were sent on mission. Jesus became the Lord through the cross, and the community has to extend that experience, sharing the risen Christ, bringing the world into the church. Mission and diakonia in the world must be rooted in faith and nourished by the eucharist.

The ministry of the bishop. In Orthodox ecclesiology, the main (though not exclusive) structure of apostolicity is the ministry of the bishop, who is concerned for the integrity and unity of both the local and the universal church.[2] In the Orthodox tradition this ministry of serving local and universal unity cannot be conceived apart from the liturgical context of the celebration of the eucharist as a sacrament of unity. The pastoral responsibility of the bishop is inseparable from the eucharist, which is nourishment for the people.

It is from this perspective that the Orthodox consider the ministry of the bishop of Rome in the structure of the church universal. While the ecclesiastical organization of Western Christianity around the authority of the bishop of Rome may have its pastoral merits (and is in any case an historical reality), the ecclesiological meaning of the organization of autonomous, autocephalous local churches, despite its failures to coordinate dispersed efforts, is the expression of the communion among local bishops in different parts of the world. Thus for the Orthodox, any eventual communion with the pope as bishop of Rome would be within the context of the normal communion of bishops of local churches.

In fact, in the liturgy the local church commemorates the primates of all local churches as a sign of communion and solidarity of the whole church universal, which is presented to Christ, who unites it with God. We are united in Christ's act of obedience to his Father on the cross. In obeying Jesus Christ, who is the same yesterday, today and forever (Heb. 13:8), the church fulfils its unity.

Christian ethics and moral community

Liturgy challenges Christian ethics which remain at the level of formal principles without touching the depths of life. It makes clear that the transformation of life which is at the heart of the gospel is not possible without communion with the bread of life.

The incarnation confers on every human being a link with Christ by the fact that he assumed our humanity. Because the human being becomes coexistent with eternity through participation in God's humanity, St Paul insists on penitence as a condition for partaking of the communion; and this is why the Orthodox tradition makes a connection between confession of sins and communion of the eucharist. Absolution, however, is not a mechanical act by the priest, but rather a matter of appropriating the power of the word of God (the first part of the liturgy), of not giving Christ a kiss as Judas did, but of imitating the thief on the cross who dared to confess his faith in public, in the presence of the authorities. Thus the eucharistic liturgy includes rituals, symbols and gestures of accepting, treating and healing each other: "Having prayed for the unity of the faith and for the communion of the Holy Spirit, let us commit ourselves, one another and our whole life to God." The celebrant, who acts on behalf of Christ and of the church, wears distinctive clothes as symbols of this office. The faithful are fully involved in the liturgical dialogue, singing and reciting, not just saying "Amen" after the prayers. Unfortunately, the traditional language and chants are not always understandable, and the symbolism of certain acts and objects and rites has become obscure.

The practice of making intercessions for one another and for all the churches projects a vision of the catholicity of the church of Christ which rejects discrimination against persons and groups within and outside the church and disregard for other nations, cultures and races.

One of the valuable insights to emerge from recent ecumenical reflection on the fundamental relation between *koinonia* and ethics, between moral life and community, is that "the community of disciples rather than the individual Christian is the bearer of the tradition and the form and matrix of the moral life. Christian ethics, in this perspective, becomes the reflection on the life of the community in the context and the perspective on the problems of human life in general."[3]

Communio in sacris

"Holy gifts to the holy people". Holy communion comes to the people as a gift, and they should accept it in gratitude. Those who offer the gifts are invited to become one in Christ. The actual sharing of holy communion, however, differs from church to church.

In the Orthodox tradition, the spiritual requirement for the members is an active participation in the liturgy in a spirit of prayer and *metanoia*. A common confession of sins is built into the structure of the liturgy. Everyone who participates is invited to share the communion. The only impediments making someone unworthy are unbelief, passivity or lack of reconciliation and love. However, there is a wide range of opinion regarding the extension of eucharistic "hospitality" to the faithful of non-Orthodox churches. First of all, the old canons made a distinction between "schismatics", who in spite of their separation remain within the church universal, and "heretics", who deny the integrity of the apostolic faith and the oneness of the church. While the baptism and ordination of the former are recognized as valid, eucharistic communion is suspended until visible union is re-established. Today, for example, theological dialogues are preparing the way for renewed eucharistic communion between Eastern and Oriental Orthodox churches. Against the heretics, who are visibly outside the church but not indifferent to it, there is sometimes formal excommunication.

The fact that the Orthodox have not shared the eucharist with other churches must be understood properly by both Orthodox and other churches. The church must protect the "mystery" of the sacrament of eucharist, but any manifestation of exclusion or exclusiveness in doing so — which has in fact too often been the tendency — is a sin against the essential purpose of the eucharist. The point is to recognize the reality of the new life we receive in the eucharist, which transforms the very being of the faithful and of the community through the power of prayer and of the Holy Spirit, who changes old creation into new. Where do we find our church and eucharist in one another's churches and liturgies? Can we affirm what is common to our traditions, following the signs of visible unity rather than trying to excuse or validate sinful situations by focusing on "things that divide the church"?

Given that the issue of eucharistic communion is at the heart of a divided Christianity, the question regarding proposals to extend "eucharistic hospitality" is whether this can feed us as pilgrims on the ecumenical journey or whether this only draws us more deeply into ancient confessional divisions? But this does not justify us in yielding to the temptation to avoid ecumenically difficult questions:

> In the context of a growing common Christian intercession, witness, service and theological convergence, and in the face of a revival of ancient denominationalism, Christians must remember that the eucharist is the cornerstone of their life together as members of one universal church. One test of ecumenical life is to renew the effort to overcome the obstacles to full concelebrated eucharist. This is an essential condition for the credibility of our ecumenical movement; while it is not there, the whole building of ecumenical witness is unsure.[4]

Theology and worship

The Orthodox have constantly underlined the relationship between theology and spirituality, between theology and contemplation. The real theologian is the one who prays, who lives in a profound and personal communion with God, in the light of God's uncreated energies. The liturgical-sacramental perspective can point to coherence and integrity in the churches' diverse theologies regarding how the church is maintained in the truth of the gospel and confessional fidelity to the local churches.

For the Roman Catholic tradition, the dogmatic pronouncements of the magisterium guarantee the right explanation of doctrines, which is obligatory for the faith. For example, the doctrine of the primacy of the bishop of Rome in the church universal becomes for Catholics "a matter of faith". In the past, this magisterial way has bypassed the participation of the people in the formulation of dogma.

Some Protestant traditions place the strongest emphasis on the Holy Scriptures as the norm of the tradition and of the life of the church. The explanation of the Bible is the task of professors of theology — the "doctors of the church". But the plurality of opinions and schools of thought greatly reduces the possibility of consensus regarding the content of the message. The great diversity found in the New Testament itself allows only some convergences, and indeed some Protestants reject the concept of consensus precisely on this ground.

In other traditions, including the Oriental churches and some Reformed and Methodist bodies, prayers, hymns and songs also play a very important role in the expression of faith.

The conciliar, liturgical way holds together the understanding of the teaching ministry of the bishop and the church as a whole — both being in continuity with the apostolic community — and the ministry of the celebration of the eucharist. When the bishop celebrates in and through liturgy, he is both transmitting the tradition and being submitted to it (which is why he confesses his faith before ordination). In this way, the liturgy makes a link between the continuous presence of Christ in the community and the continuity of the witness of the apostles.

Liturgical renewal

By enabling the people to participate in the celebration with the whole range of human faculties and senses, the liturgy embraces the great variety of ways in which human life is sanctified. But if participation in the liturgy and the "liturgy after the liturgy" is to realize its constructive potential in the life of the churches and ecumenically, the need for liturgical renewal is evident. We have already remarked on one evidence of this need for renewal: the contradiction between the "insider's" language used in Orthodox worship for liturgical prayers, hymns and Bible readings, and the language used for communicating with society at large. More broadly, the rigidity of the rites and ceremonies can suffocate the living rhythm of the liturgy, and its beauty may be obscured by the heavy symbolism attached to objects and gestures.

Another contradiction results from the enclosure of the altar by the iconostasis. This tempts the priest to read the main prayer, including the epiclesis, inaudibly, depriving the faithful of a central part of the liturgy and running counter to the essence of the service itself, which is meant to be read and chanted aloud by priest and people, singing, crying, shouting the triumphal hymn, "Holy, holy, holy..." A more general polarity between clergy and people, which fails to recognize the common vocation of the *laos*, the people of God, is thus reinforced. It is precisely in order to avoid turning the liturgy into a clerical action that ordination takes place in and through the community. Liturgical renewal should thus aim at a greater involvement of the whole people of God, women and men, in many forms of worship, especially in congregational singing and sharing:

> For too long the very term *laikos* carried with it connotations of passivity, of not belonging to the active, i.e. *clerical*, stratum in the church. But we know

that initially the term meant the *belonging* to the *laos*, the people of God, to "a chosen generation, royal priesthood, a holy nation, a peculiar people" which God "has called out of darkness into his marvellous light" (1 Pet. 2:9). We know that in the sacraments of baptism and holy chrismation each member of the church was made into the temple of the Holy Spirit, dedicated, consecrated to God and called to serve him. We know, in other terms, that each *laikos* is above all called to be a witness, i.e. an active participant in the church's mission in the world.[5]

At the centre of liturgical renewal is the question of the participation of the people of God in the eucharist:

> No revival of the parish as a truly liturgical community fulfilling itself at Christ's table in his kingdom is possible without a eucharistic revival, which alone can give life and integrate with one another the gifts and charisms of all members of the body of Christ.[6]

In fact the Orthodox have historically attached a great value to the plurality of forms and expressions of liturgical art and spirituality. Some churches need to be reminded of the old practice of using a variety of liturgies whose styles reflect the missionary milieu and culture of the participants.

But new prayers are also needed. In private and in corporate worship, Christians ought to make mention of the specific needs of society, national, regional and global, and in this way keep in touch with the everyday needs of the rest of the community. A collection of prayers should be developed, keeping in mind the special needs of contemporary society. The role of worship within the whole range of human culture and in all varieties of human creativity must be rediscovered: church music, iconography, liturgical art, hymnography — taking care, of course, to avoid false inculturation and contextualization.

Beyond this, new forms of worship should be developed for mobile populations, travellers, children and young people, people in industry, foreigners, refugees, non-Christians in the vicinity of our congregations — all of whom have no permanent roots. New forms of community outside existing parishes should be established in view of the different needs of these types of people. To make parish worship more comprehensible and inviting to young people, for example, special services or catechetical explanation could precede the liturgy.

The Orthodox have always been concerned about the unity of all churches and of the whole of humankind in the liturgical services. If this principle of intercession and prayer for others becomes central to parish worship, the church can go beyond a superficial understanding of the unity of church and world, and so realize the vision of the liturgical orientation of Christian life eloquently expressed by a recent ecumenical consultation:

> All creation bears the stamp of holy things. The church, in its whole bearing, should, as a moral community, help to foster a "sacramental" orientation towards life, just as the church understands itself, its being, its mission and witness on a sacramental and eucharistic basis. There is no better place to begin than with the moral meaning of the sacraments themselves. Baptism, for example, is at the heart of the church in so far as the baptized become the effective witness — martyr — to gospel values in the world. Questions of faith and moral and social questions are inseparable from the act of Christian witness that baptism mandates. Eucharist as a sacrament of communion... is real food for a scattered people in their moral struggle, to heal the brokenness of human being and community. The church sees both its inner unity and solidarity with others as expressions of sharing the bread of life. The sacraments as person-shaping rites can lead us to sacramental living.[7]

NOTES

1. Cf. Gennadios Limouris, "Nicene Creed", in *Dictionary of the Ecumenical Movement*, pp.727-28.

2. Cf. Emilianos Timiadis, *Lectures on Orthodox Ecclesiology*, 2 vols, Joensuu, Finland, Joensuun Yliopiston, 1992; Ion Bria, "Challenges to the Orthodox Ecclesiology in the New European Situation", in Pobee, ed., *Construction of a Common European Home*, pp.81-86.

3. *Costly Unity*, Geneva, WCC, 1993, pp.91.

4. Ion Bria, "Reflections on Mission Theology and Methodology", *loc. cit.*, p.69.

5. *Orthodox Thought*, p.63; cf. I. Bria, ed., *People Hunger to be Near to God*, Geneva, WCC, 1991, pp.56-66.

6. *Go Forth in Peace*, p.44.

7. *Costly Unity*, pp.88-89.

4. Gospel and Culture and Liturgy

Orthodox theology and missiology have several important contributions to offer to the ongoing ecumenical discussion of gospel and culture. Let me mention three key insights and then seek to illustrate these with reference to a critical contemporary gospel-culture encounter — that centering on the recent experience of Orthodox churches in Eastern and Central Europe.

In the first place, the Orthodox make a connection between the revelation of God and the gospel, because the same *Logos* of God spoke through the Old Testament prophets and was manifested as a human person in Jesus Christ. During his ministry Jesus Christ created the circle of the apostles by teaching the truth with power; at Pentecost he created the community of the church around the apostles by sending on them the Holy Spirit as the Spirit of Truth. The proclamation of the gospel and the teaching of the apostolic doctrine are not two disconnected realities. This is illustrated during the liturgy when the worshipping community, after proclaiming the presence of Christ — "Christ is in our midst" — must confess, "You are the Christ, the son of the living God" (Matt. 16:16).

For the Orthodox, then, in any debate about gospel and culture the *content* of the gospel, the *lex credendi*, must be recognized through those who have the Spirit to discern it — the saints.

Second, this integrity is expressed in the tradition, which is thus a critical principle for assuming human culture. The tradition is the gospel retained through its reception in and by the confessing community. It carries the memory of the history of salvation in New Testament times and anticipates the kingdom of God. For the Orthodox, the tradition is a way to protect publicly the mystery of God revealed in the scriptures against the inroads of "another gospel". This tradition means both fidelity and continuity: the given content of the gospel is not broken into pieces.

Third, cultures can be seen as representing the "anointed feet" of the gospels, as the apostles were of Christ. Or, to change the image, as the gospel moves in various times and places, culture represents the cosmos with open arms receiving the descent of the Holy Spirit (as in the icon of Pentecost). The culture itself has to be converted and baptized in order to assume the gospel. In handling the "syntax" of gospel and culture, "contextual theology" must pair them in a sacramental and not a syncretistic way. More clarity is needed about those positions and typologies which create real hindrances to the mutual understanding and credibility of the churches in their mission and common witness.

In applying these insights to the situation of the Orthodox churches in Central and Eastern Europe after the fall of communist governments, we must begin by acknowledging that it is impossible to make a completely adequate presentation of what a new movement for mission would mean today for these churches. Certain studies and surveys indicate that new developments are taking place, especially in the field of religious instruction and theological education in public schools and universities. Faculties of theology are now being reintegrated into public universities, and women have access to theological formation. Nevertheless, many superficial and misleading descriptions of the missionary understanding and attitude of these churches persist, including the venerable stereotype of Orthodoxy in Eastern Europe as withdrawn into liturgical, nationalistic and cultural isolation and uninterested in evangelism.[1] To this is added the charge that the Orthodox churches are so preoccupied with the struggles against the proselyting crusades of foreign Protestant groups, the "new evangelization" in their territory by Roman Catholic societies and the efforts of Greek Catholic (uniate) churches to reclaim properties and privileges lost during the communist period that they are unable to respond to the missionary challenge before them. The insinuation is that this attitude is grounded in their nationalism, supported by a new generation of nationalist politicians.

One would hope that those within the ecumenical movement who offer political analyses of the situation of the churches of Eastern Europe might moderate their harshest criticisms for the sake of common understanding.[2] It is a matter of ecumenical courtesy and discipline not to invent arbitrary grounds for charging the Orthodox with ignorance and irresponsibility about their own theology and practice of mission and instead to pursue the search for common witness even in a controversial context. Moreover, the situation in the Orthodox churches in the Balkans is especially complex; and one needs a fairly detailed acquaintance with them if one is to speak about them realistically.

Nor is it evident that these churches need lessons in the "evangelization of the unreached" from Western churches, Protestant or Roman Catholic. The Orthodox have a vivid memory of the historic Western Christian missionary strategies in such lands as Ukraine, Moravia and Transylvania. The Orthodox have a different understanding of the apostolic mission of the church, "the church of nations". They speak about local church-based evangelism and liturgical synaxis as the springboard for mission in the world.[3] They have used an Eastern methodology to conceptualize and describe the history of Christianity, and ask to be respected for the richness they add to Christian culture through their *martyria* — not only oral proclamation of the gospel but also *martyrdom* following the steps of the crucified Christ.

The "communist world" has been considered a special social and political category, a world that rejected the gospel and divided Christians. The Stalinist era certainly dislocated Christian faith and culture, but through their discreet and silent liturgical resistance the Orthodox have made their own contribution to the collapse of communism, which they consider as a real revolution. They know better than anyone else the pain of transition in the post-communist era. Not only is it unfair to accuse them of lacking a sense of revolution and longing to return to the pre-communist period, but such changes also cultivate an ideology which maintains the Christian divisions in Europe on political terms: uniting Europe is identified solely with Western Christendom, excluding the Orthodox citizens of formerly communist countries.

The ecumenical movement helped these Orthodox churches to cross a long period of restrictions and violence. In coming to rely on the intercessions and solidarity of all the member churches of the World Council of Churches, a conciliar fellowship of which the Protestant churches are an integral part, they have learned much about praying for unity, eucharistic hospitality, renewal, common witness, spirituality. While it is scandalous that some voices within Orthodox churches now dismiss all Western churches as heretical sects, it is equally scandalous that some Protestant churches have supported fundamentalist groups who are seeking the growth of the church in Eastern Europe by making "new-born Christians" of baptized Orthodox Christians.

What is needed for a relevant mission movement in the new gospel and culture context confronting the Orthodox churches in Eastern Europe?

1. The first necessary condition is to regulate the political discipline of the churches by re-evaluating the terms of church-state relationships and religious legislation.

In order to survive the communist period, the Orthodox accepted an equivocal symphony with the state, a fragile agreement which acknowledged the existence of the church as a *religious institution* but rejected its calling as a *movement for mission*. After many decades of bearing this cross, the churches have not yet found the courage to declare their strict separation from the state.[4] Paradoxically, some Orthodox voices have even after the revolution expressed nostalgia for the old "symphony" and suggested that such an arrangement might be restored with the new regimes. In some quarters, indeed, a new state-church alliance is proclaimed as a divine institution; for example, there have been calls to restore "Holy Russia" as the "third Rome". Against the stream of European history, there is still a pious veneration of national conformism in Eastern Europe.

But this is far from the whole story. Liberated to organize their life and mission apart from an unfavourable and oppressive church-state framework, various church institutions, Christian bodies and missionary associations recognize clearly what a stumbling block it would be to their mission to remain under the tutelage of the state. With the national state no longer determining the orientations of its evangelistic witness and religious instruction, the church is also free to propose various forms of cohabitation with the state — symphony, autonomy, separation, partnership, establishment — according to the essential aspects of its existence. As a result of the revolution, the church, called to give full account of the faith it has received from the apostles and to transmit the retained tradition, can fully affirm its identity and openly discern the strategy to fulfil its mission.

2. "Orthodoxy" is a word that is used in many different senses. An integrist stream has emerged in the aftermath of the revolution which considers that part of the struggle for identity is to teach a strict Orthodoxy, calling for a conversion to "the true faith" and "the true church". One group even speaks about an elitist Orthodoxy, represented by those who "remained faithful to the gospel" during the time of communist violence against the church. It insists on a strict observance of the canons and an exaggerated ritualism which suffocates the simplicity of the gospel and the essential eucharistic substance of the liturgy.

This is not, however, the only version of what constitutes exact adherence to the Orthodox faith. What should not be lost sight of, however, is the context in which this diversity arises: the profound ignorance of tradition and liturgy in the several generations which grew up after the war, particularly among young people in large cities. The great majority of the people is no longer able to identify what or where the tradition is. There is an amalgam of faith convictions, cultural assumptions and national prejudices, but the loss of traditional values has dispossessed people of their identity and way of life. They are like strangers in a foreign land, disoriented, disillusioned and hopeless.

In order to bring back the tradition in the memory of the young people, the churches have established various programmes: to intensify catechetical teaching, to teach religion in public schools. What is wrong with teaching the true faith, Orthodoxy?

> We are to be answerable to the world for our belief and our actions. We have the obligation to explain to people what we believe and what we do not believe, why we act in a certain way and not in other ways. Christians are not obliged to do what others tell us but we are under obligation to explain our convictions and actions. By so doing, we affirm our Christian identity and at the same time strengthen our ties with others outside the church.[5]

The Orthodox realize that the transmission of the faith cannot be taken for granted as an automatic consequence of an uninterrupted historical apostolic succession. Both militant atheism and secularism have pointed to the breaking of the tradition. They also understand that without a personal confession of faith there is no living church. Faith is always personal and relational. There is no baptism, no liturgy, no eucharistic communion unless the faithful personally repeat the baptismal confession of faith: "I believe."

We must recognize the place of the Orthodox faith in the tradition of these churches. It is here that they find the memory of the history of salvation. The pilgrimage of the church bearing the apostolic witness constitutes its mission; and rejecting this content of faith means undermining that mission. This is why Roman Catholic or Protestant mission among the Orthodox inevitably comes as a call to substitute, to adapt or to change their faith. Doctrinal fidelity for them means precisely integrity to Christ and to the content of the gospel.

3. Within the notion of tradition there is no clear distinction between gospel and culture. For most Orthodox churches, the memory of God is assumed into the memory of the origin and history of a particular nation and church. The tradition encompasses both integrity to the apostolic faith and the cultural context of that faith, that is, its reception in personal faith and cultural expressions by a human community converted to Christ.

As we said, the Orthodox today are obliged to speak about a forgotten and lost tradition. At what level is the failure — at the level of personal faith, institutional visibility, social influence, economic privilege, cultural creativity?

We said that the two dimensions of the church — as ecclesial institution and as movement for mission — were disconnected under communism. Since the revolution the churches have seen their main task as reinforcing their institutional visibility, regaining their national status, obtaining more public space for mission. Nearly all of them have concentrated their efforts on the construction or restoration of church buildings as places of worship. Those worried about the state of spiritual life in the churches, especially the missionary associations, have criticized this priority, but it is argued that the faithful need a visible and tangible sign, a symbolic place to rediscover their identity as people of God. On this understanding church building is not a mere human construction; it is a symbol of divine presence.

The shortage of places to worship is in fact a serious impediment to mission. But the most dramatic consequence of the violent totalitarian system, apart from the ignorance of the faith and of the liturgy on the part of young people, is the trivialization of Christian culture, a kind of bastard offspring of Byzantine ecclesiastical philosophy and Marxist ideology. This is a fundamental crisis in the whole history of Orthodoxy, since the people have lost a reference point for self-identity. Unaware of the depth of this crisis, the churches have undertaken a series of contradictory projects. Some believe that the evangelistic witness today can still rely on the heritage of traditional Christian culture. The Russian church still uses the Old Slavonic as a liturgical language, claiming this as a sacred pattern:

> On the one hand, in many churches, through the old biblical and liturgical texts a national language and cultures were shaped and still protected. On the other, the old liturgical language limits the very possibilities of the contemporary faithful to identify themselves with the liturgy which is their prayer, and handicaps the church in communicating with the younger generation.[6]

The gospel has to be proclaimed and taught in every generation, in its own language and symbols. It cannot be appropriated once for all by a particular culture; it has to be liberated for new connections and new praxis.

This cultural conformism is reinforced by the presence of foreign evangelists, local fundamentalist groups, esoteric religions and other missionary agencies. The evangelical streams proclaim a clear and strict message which makes no approach to the predominant culture of society or the establishment in which the existing churches seem to be trapped. Both the traditional culture and the traditional liturgical life are disregarded in favour of personal faith and conversion, which is not determined by a particular creed. Such proselytism among the Orthodox is therefore not iconoclastic, in the sense that it is not seeking to replace the old culture. By contrast, the campaign for a new evangelization in Europe under the authority of the Roman Catholic Church is a more offensive form of proselytism because it is based on a claim to rectify the tradition of faith and the history of the Orthodox churches, and accordingly to change the old national culture.

The weakness of these new missionary developments is that the evangelistic witness made is not in harmony with the cultural and intellectual ferment which is challenging the old mixture of religion and ideology and creating new concepts, symbols and attitudes that will respond to the younger generation, which has no ancient Christian heritage and no longer carries the baggage of that heritage either. This disparity and disconnection are the stumbling blocks to the extension of the gospel in the society at large. The traditional culture is still viewed as a symbolic identity to be protected against any threats. Therefore, the cost of a living tradition is high: some things must be retained, some things must be let go. But the church has to find a common language and symbols to communicate and affirm what it believes, renewing the credal and confessional propositions so that they can be received by a new community.

4. The most difficult task for the church to face is the disintegration of human community reflected in new divisions in society and the dislocation of families. The disconnection of the tradition from social and cultural reality has led to the loss of a sense of moral community and the disorganization of the koinonia which is at the heart of human community. Society becomes an agglomeration of individuals and smaller communities, which cannot reconstitute a coherent social body because of economic poverty, corruption, violence and even civil war.

At this point the dynamics of liturgy can come to the aid of the Orthodox. The eucharistic liturgy is for them not only a missionary event but a metaphor of human existence and community. It is a missionary event because it manifests Jesus Christ, whom the faithful confess, invoke and worship.

The "liturgical model" typology is based on the ecclesiology of koinonia, the communion of local churches united in an act of faith and worship which transcends the particular identity of any of them. Yet these identities are not lost; therefore, there is no need to propose a detachment of the Christians from their ethnic identities as something destructive. Rather, these identities are baptized, transfigured and incorporated into the catholicity of the church, which is neither a cultural uniformity nor a multinational community of separate ethnic entities, but a koinonia of autocephalous churches (an autocephalous church is the church of one particular *place*, whether national or multinational). It is the *local church* which creates culture in the process of reception and transmission of the gospel as worship, order, ethos and spirituality. Culture is not an independent, anonymous construct. Every local church, every nation has its own cultural configuration.

The liturgical model is also based on the sharing of ministry and responsibility within the church. For as we have seen, the eucharistic liturgy does not allow discrimination between hierarchy and people (*laos*) or rich and poor. The eucharist shows that the whole life of the church depends on the invocation of the Holy Spirit in the presence of the community, Christ being in their midst. No one is independent in the liturgy. The transcendence of the risen Christ, the invocation of the Holy Spirit, the participation of the people who confess their faith and bring the gifts — all these constitute the koinonia, vertical and horizontal. To be sure, this typology is not immune from distortion; worship can be spoiled by ritualism, veneration of symbols, absence of communion in the eucharist. The hierarchy can co-opt the authority and neglect the participation of the people, turning the church into a clerical institution.

The liturgical typology can also influence political life, both in terms of the relationship between state and church and of Christian identity and religious pluralism. The local church, if it is a "national" or "majority" church, should not have a monopoly on the power in a country. In the name of the catholicity of the church and ecumenical discipline, it should establish a partnership — a critical symphony — with the state, leaving space for other churches. Many have spoken about certain countries in terms of their "Orthodox identity" or about Europe in terms of its "Christian identity". The ecclesiology of koinonia challenges such ideas with its deep sense of catholicity, which overcomes both division and uniformity of identities, whether confessional or ethnic.

5. Fifty years after the second world war, the church has to face critical questions regarding its own political attitudes during the years of communist rule. European history reminds us of many forms of idolatry perpetrated when tradition functions to control the gospel instead of protecting it. Some groups now push the churches to ask forgiveness, in a spirit of repentance and reconciliation, for their failure to demonstrate gospel values in the historical and cultural traditions in which the memory of God is not transparent. Others criticize the church today for failing to

turn back to God and to follow the crucified Christ in all that has happened in recent history. The churches' mistakes have created victims, from whom the church must demand pardon.

What is needed is once again to place in the centre of history and culture the memory, the remembrance of God, and to entrust the future of the church into God's hands. For a repentant community which confesses the violations for which it is responsible, a new beginning is always possible. In an earlier chapter we quoted extensively from Nicholas Cabasilas' explanation of the liturgy; in his other well-known work, *The Life in Christ*, he writes:

> After Jesus returned to life he received those of his friends who had continued in their purpose to share in the festal joy. He bore them no grudge for having deserted him and fled at the height of perils. So he called his disciples together and came now to them where they should assemble and meet with him. When he met them and appeared to them he did not reproach them for their flight. It does not appear anywhere that he remembered any such thing against them — how they had all affirmed that they would share death and the uttermost extremity with him, yet could not endure the thought of the terrors even before they happened. He bestowed upon them peace and the Holy Spirit and similar blessings, and then entrusted to them the care of the whole world and set them up as rulers over all the earth.
>
> These things he did to all their company. What things did he for the very leader, who had often betrayed the affection that he bore him and had denied his love? Not only did he forbear to expose his denial — he did not remind him of his pledge which he had foresworn by failing to join his Teacher in death, that pledge which he broke so short a time later — but to him, apart from the others, he sent the messengers of his resurrection and so did him honour. When he encountered him he conversed with him as befits a friend and asked him whether his love for him was greater than that of his other friends. When Peter said that he loved him, he again asked him, and when he heard him say, "I love you" [John 21:16], he again asked whether he was loved by him. He might, I think, have asked many times over, had not Peter been grieved and refused to answer further, as though there were need of many words for him who knows all things to find out that he was loved.[7]

There are many contradictions in the current movement for mission within the Orthodox churches in Eastern Europe, but it remains faithful to the spirit of their tradition, which still preserves a relevance for the identity of the people, while giving them the freedom to reinterpret that tradition. Therefore iconoclastic proselytism — which has sometimes even been accompanied by the threat of violence — is a labour in vain. The

Catholicization or Protestantization of the Orthodox is a contradiction in terms.

The liturgical model should operate critically and effectively in breaking the obstacles of language, sociology or ethos that hinder the mediation of the memory of God to the new generations. The remembrance of God, the centre of the liturgy, cannot be channelled through only one particular cultural heritage. The eucharistic liturgy has to be liberated from all cultural apprehensions, so that it may be a missionary event: the place where the church educates, teaches, anoints and nourishes its evangelists and missionaries.

The subject of gospel and cultures merits a consistent and systematic exploration. The typology underlined by the Orthodox is that of pairing of realities in a sacramental, not syncretistic way. The Reformation mind seems to be based on the dissociation of realities, a kind of "anti-transubstantiation" theology and culture. Hence the separation between state and church, the disparity between doctrine and worship, the division between evangelical faith and mystical experience. Hence liberal culture and humanism. On the contrary, the Orthodox see rather the connections: the *lex credendi* protected in the *lex orandi*, the gospel message translated into the social *corpus*, which has nothing in common with a totalitarian system, through the discipline of political critical symphony. Orthodoxy is not the result of a political game, but a way to keep the church faithful to Christ.

The new evangelization in the former communist countries is an immense task and cannot be realized exclusively by the churches of the majority. Indeed, they have a unique political role primarily towards the minorities. The existing churches have their own principles, methods, strategies and priorities in mission and evangelism. These are not by definition discriminatory and contradictory assumptions. "Called to one hope: the gospel in diverse cultures", the theme of the WCC's 1996 conference on world mission and evangelism, is a call for immediate, here-and-now common Christian witness, in order to light a new faith in old Christian countries. It is a costly witness which follows Jesus, who washed the feet of his disciples and sent them out to the whole world to preach the gospel and bestow grace on all nations. As "anointed feet of the Lord", Christian missionaries must proclaim the gospel of peace, forgiveness, reconciliation. As for those who make a counter-witness, St Paul warns, "Keep an eye on those who cause dissensions and offenses, in opposition to the teaching that you have learned; avoid them. For such people do not serve our Lord Jesus Christ, but their own appetites, and by smooth talk and flattery they deceive the hearts of the simple-minded" (Rom. 16:17f.).

NOTES

1. Cf. Ernest Benz, *The Eastern Orthodox Church: Its Thought and Life*, New York, Anchor Books, 1963, p.213.

2. Cf. Paul Mojzes, "Threats to Ecumenism in Eastern Europe", *One World*, no. 205, May 1995, pp.14-17. Articles on the churches of Eastern Europe appear regularly in the journal Mojzes edits, *Religion in Eastern Europe*, published by Christians Associated for Relations with Eastern Europe (Rosemont College, Rosemont, Pennsylvania, USA). Cf. also Raphaël Aubert, *La tentation de l'Est: Religion, pouvoir et nationalismes*, Geneva, Labor et Fides, 1991, pp.16-18.

3. On this see Ion Bria, ed., *Martyria-Mission: The Witness of Orthodox Churches Today*, and *Go Forth in Peace: Orthodox Perspectives on Mission*, Geneva, WCC, 1989; Ion Bria and Petros Vasileiadis, *Orthodox Christian Martyria*, Katerini, Tertios, 1989; Aram Keshishian, *The Christian Witness at the Crossroads in the Middle East*, Beirut, Middle East Council of Churches, 1992.

4. On the church and national identity see Ninan Koshy, *Churches in the World of Nations: International Politics and the Mission and Ministry of the Church*, Geneva, WCC, 1994, esp. ch. 5, pp.46-57.

5. Raymond Fung, *The Isaiah Vision: An Ecumenical Strategy for Congregational Evangelism*, Geneva, WCC, 1992, pp.43-44.

6. *Go Forth in Peace*, p.25.

7. Nicholas Cabasilas, *The Life in Christ*, VI, 11c.

5. *Liturgy and Common Christian Witness*

While those continuing differences which are real hindrances to mutual understanding and credibility should not be swept aside too easily, there are several areas in which the theme of the liturgy after the liturgy can offer new perspectives on certain polarizations and theological misinterpretations, including Orthodox and evangelical perceptions of each other. We have already indicated some of these divisive issues in earlier chapters; here let us point to some areas in which we can concentrate our common efforts.

1. In evangelistic witness the Orthodox are concerned not only with the *act of communication*, which raises the problem of cultural diversity and language, but also with the *content of the gospel* — with God's revelation and self-giving in Christ — which raises the problem of articulating and confessing faith in Christ. For the Orthodox, the tradition of a common Christology, articulated in a conciliar way in the 4th and 5th centuries, guarantees the integrity and continuity of the church. Can we confess together, as part of the apostolic tradition, a Christology of the true God and true man which can serve as a unifying principle for the local churches? Is the risen Christ whom we know present in the life of others? Do other churches have the means for opening themselves to the reality of the same Christ?[1] Unless we can respond positively, we will not liberate ourselves from the condemnations and anathemas of the past and find a method of treating other Christians and churches in the framework of a wide conciliarity which recognizes a diversity of specific missions. The issue of rebaptism highlights the question of the boundaries within which different expressions and practices of the apostolic tradition are acceptable. Proselytism always implies a rejection of the validity of the baptism given in another church. Could we ask that the mutual recognition of baptism be accepted as obligatory and rebaptism abandoned while the divergences which appear irreconcilable are discussed?

2. We have repeatedly emphasized that proclamation of the gospel, which is a task for all Christians, is inseparable from the celebration of the liturgy and the transmission of ministerial responsibility, for it is around the gospel and altar that the worshipping community is prepared, educated and nourished as an evangelizing community. Within this fellowship some have a distinctive calling to a discipleship which may demand an intensified personal identity with and loyalty to Christ. A number of teaching and

evangelizing ministries have emerged in the tradition: pastor, priest, teacher, theologian, bishop, evangelist, prophet. But tradition does not specify limits to the materials and media to be used in communicating the gospel message, requiring only that they be appropriate to the nature of mission. Could we interpret the tradition as being concerned with other kinds of agents, transmission and communication — exceptional charismatic reminders, missionaries and evangelists? Is there sufficient ground in the tradition for taking as comprehensive as possible a view of those who are *Christophoroi* ("bearers of Christ") and *synergoi* ("co-workers") with God? The church must then recognize and develop the gifts of the people, integrating them into its total mission, encouraging some and perhaps restraining others.

3. Orthodox attitudes and mission strategy have depended too heavily on the "ecumenical" interests of the large ecclesiastical centres and on the nationalistic aims of local political leaders. The resulting mixture of Christian theology, political ideology and national culture has limited the "catholicity" of the church. Orthodoxy is larger and more inclusive than the frontiers of the fifteen or sixteen local churches within which it is presented. Without giving up the cultural tradition which indicates the peregrination of the gospel in various times and places and constitutes the memory of the local people, we need a rereading of history.

In this pilgrimage, we have seen, the church has made various forms of alliances with states. While many of the faithful and especially the hierarchy believe that a complete separation between state and church would diminish the church's cultural and missionary influence, a clear political autonomy is required, not only to maintain the necessary distinction between ethics and politics but also to give the church the freedom to raise its voice on behalf of the gospel against political powers. The church has to defend what is necessary for the koinonia of the community in the church and in society. It needs space to protect the memory, which gives identity, space to worship the Lord of history, space to hope in the coming of the kingdom of God, especially today, when political powers struggle to control the lives of people.

Behind all the debates about Christian mission in the contemporary world lies the personal Christian experience of the faithful. Ecumenical fellowship is not just about making our own experience better understood by other Christian communities. All Christian communities, large and small, should have the privilege of giving and receiving, receiving and giving, from out of their convictions and experiences. All should become more sensitive to the diverse forms and strategies of evangelism. The recognition that no one is untouched by God's gift and call makes possible an exchange and reconciliation of gifts which the Holy Spirit has offered and offers to other churches.

4. The liturgy after the liturgy never involves coercion, manipulation or marginalization, but mutual respect, complementarity and rigorous observance of the freedom of religion of others. The question of the nature and limits of religious liberty has been underscored by the presence of foreign missionaries in Orthodox countries. We have seen in the previous chapters that these arrogant and powerful efforts to change the people's church affiliation, sometimes even including "financial incentives" or the threat of violence to win converts, is ecumenically unacceptable. But in assessing the movement of people between churches, the local Orthodox churches should not ignore the criticisms of those who have left their ranks nor blame any Christian for his or her church affiliation. Each person must feel joyful, sound and settled in his or her local Christian community; after all, there is something universal in each local church, for "all of you are one in Christ Jesus" (Gal. 3:28).

The call to a common life in Christ and common Christian witness requires going beyond the futile and indeed dangerous polarizations and confrontations created by competitive evangelism and systematic proselytism. Ecumenism is a challenge to comfortably installing ourselves in sinful sectarianism and integrism. We must rediscover the importance of global unity and common Christian witness. Where common witness is not possible because of apparently irreconcilable interpretations of the gospel or experiences and perceptions of culture and society, dialogue should nevertheless continue, in order to discover whether these positions are church-dividing or can be overcome.

5. We cannot be indifferent to the demands of persons for truth and meaning, their need for personal faith and loving communion, their aspirations for the integrity and totality of human being and living. More and more the course of history ignores the mystery of God. How can we proclaim Christ in a society in which politics controls the life of the people and economic laws and social norms ignore the values of the gospel, a society in which the weak and excluded have no prospects?

St Paul says about the ministry of the apostles: "Think of us in this way, as servants of Christ and stewards of God's mysteries" (1 Cor. 4:1); "we are God's servants, working together (*synergoi*)" (1 Cor. 3:9). Following the apostles, the church understands and fulfils its mission by responding to particular situations, though its endeavours always remain partial and imperfect. The difficult challenges of today require a renewal of the churches' common evangelistic witness. The evangelicals point to a lack of spirituality as a chronic weakness of the historic established churches and emphasize that the salvation of society calls for persons of faith. The Orthodox church holds up the example of evangelizing local communities which, by confessing Christ and breaking the bread, maintain the links which unite everyone. One day the working of each builder will become visible, because they have a common purpose. But "neither the one who plants nor the one who waters is anything, but only God who gives the growth" (1 Cor. 3:7).

The "new evangelization" in Europe

Recent discussions of the "new evangelization" in Europe, stimulated by several official Roman Catholic documents, raise particular issues of common witness which should be considered within the framework of contemporary ecumenical missiology.[2] Without entering into a global analysis of this idea, let us suggest some points at which the Orthodox churches can enter into this debate, some possibilities for ecumenical cooperation and some critical observations.

The Orthodox must at least say whether this theme and programme are not too ambitious and costly for them, given their missionary resources and their agenda already too full of insurmountable problems: civil wars, economic underdevelopment, the elaboration of democracy, immigration crises, fear for the future. At the same time, they must not allow themselves to be overwhelmed by their weakness. Every new form of united Christian witness can highlight the ecumenical understanding and worldwide solidarity which have been developing over several decades.

The "new evangelization" in Europe is perceived as an ecumenical undertaking.[3] Ecumenism in the context of "new evangelization" is a new language, whose importance must be recognized. Cooperation between Catholics and Orthodox is seen as indispensable, and those who have drawn up this programme have made a remarkable effort to underline the ecclesiological and historical bases of such cooperation. For example, the West and the East are said to constitute the "two lungs" of the universal church. "These two immense traditions," says Pope John Paul II, "although different, belong to one another. Together they form Christian Europe, both past and present."[4] Both from the Orthodox and Roman Catholic sides it has been said that the "new evangelization" can and should be developed on the basis of an ecclesiology of communion, the ecclesiology of "sister churches". The pope himself has emphasized that "the fact that we say 'sister churches' is not only a convenient phrase, but a fundamental ecumenical category of ecclesiology".[5]

One must ask whether the theological dialogue between Catholics and Orthodox, delayed and tortuous in comparison with the development of the ecumenical movement as a whole, is sufficiently rooted in our two churches to lay the foundations for a programme of evangelization in Europe. In reality, it would seem that the timid results of this dialogue have not really triggered a response, that nothing has been definitely achieved and that it needs very little in the way of non-theological factors to destabilize the bilateral agreements that do exist.

A new language must be found for East-West dialogue. In practice, all the anti-ecumenical and proselytizing currents arise out of attitudes towards the ecclesial status of others, expressed in the first instance, as we saw earlier, by the rejection of baptism. Where the validity of the other's baptism is not recognized, it is the very nature of the church, which is constituted by the rite of Christian initiation, that is at stake.[6]

While the Catholics (as is evident from the pope's comment cited above) have a deep interest in mutual recognition as "sister churches", this terminology has not yet been widely accepted in the East, and from the Orthodox side there is no reciprocity. In the end, what is this all about? Can we in fact believe that the two ecclesiologies, the two ways of looking at the church, can co-exist when we know the inflexibility of both churches in ecclesiological matters? Does it mean that the two are churches in the true sense, by their fidelity to the apostolic faith and the tradition of the ecumenical church, the visible expression of the *Una Sancta*? Are the Orthodox then mistaken in fearing that the doctrinal status of the "separated Easterners" is being promulgated without their involvement and that the condition of Orthodoxy is seen as that of a "wounded church"?[7] Or is this mutual recognition only a question of diplomacy, aiming at a better global ecclesiastical organization? If so, this should be acknowledged openly. Certainly the phrase "sister church" has symbolic value for expressing the healing of memories, mutual forgiveness, a common witness of solidarity, the burial of proselytism and useless polemics and the cold war. But to reduce the ecumenism of today to a simple reinstatement of history would be a serious mistake.

Despite all the ambiguities in how the Orthodox feel about the Catholics and vice versa (for their faults are similar), some of their strong common convictions can be and are being expressed in both practical commitments and symbolic gestures: Bible translation and distribution, initiation into liturgical life, spirituality, training of youth and students, the search for a common date for Easter, veneration of saints, reciprocal interchurch aid, missions of reconciliation in national or ethnic conflict. Ecumenism is increasingly moving beyond the sphere of bishops and theologians to become the source of on-the-spot concrete witness by the faithful.

Forever to make ecclesiological comparisons between East and West is to fall into a dreadful trap. What we *can* do is to acknowledge the value of the historic and specific mission of each church, in its own area where it has lived and still lives. When we talk of exchange of ecumenical talents, of awareness and reconciliation of the gifts the Holy Spirit offers to different churches, we are speaking a new language which leaves room for pastoral missions adapted to different situations. In fact it has to do with reconciling the proclamation of the gospel among the nations by legitimate but particular missions which, for all their diversity and even contradictions, have built up the universal church. Here the Orthodox must abandon the evasive attitude they have long adopted towards the vocation of those who do not belong to their own church and become more open to a reading of the history of non-Orthodox churches as expressing the same desire to share the good news in diverse situations.

Instead of wrapping up their irreconcilable ecclesiological divergencies in neat parcels, the two churches must put these convictions on the table openly and unpack them, in a spirit of conciliarity. At all costs, what Nikos Nissiotis called "dangerous ecclesiological misunderstandings" must be avoided. For example, the Catholic Church would seem to want us to understand that ecumenism is linked to a *Western* model of institutional unity. This dependence on a model which supplants the other traditions, and which thereby excludes conciliarity, does not help in the understanding of ecumenism today, particularly in view of the fact that the abuse of this Western Roman model in an earlier "ecumenical movement" in the East created one of the most intolerable forms of counter-witness — namely, uniatism.

The fact is that one must go to work again to renew the lost conciliarity. A dialogue must be initiated which respects the ecumenical discipline and the critiques coming from the Orthodox and all the other perspectives within the universal church, in which we can think together and be nourished by a common vision of unity. This vision must be constantly expressed and allowed gradually to spread among all Christians. As long as West and East recognize each other as traditions securely anchored in conciliarity, there are neither irreconcilable positions between the two churches nor endless critical confrontations.

Europe is not an empty terrain, but it is a new field in the eyes of Christians. In a secularized society the two churches find themselves in serious missionary difficulties. In the East the return of the religious element to public life is ambiguous. All sorts of liberal improvizations of the "New Age" are being proclaimed without discrimination in the name of religion. In the West, the indifference towards God in general and Christianity in particular is barren and without nuances, leading to frightening fragmentation of the image of Christianity.

Faced with the "religionless society" created by the positive reception of secularization, the two churches together can declare that history and human society are relative values compared with the values of the gospel, compared with the God who dwells within and among us, compared with the ultimate transfiguration through the resurrection. The communist ideology tried to draw a sharp line of demarcation between faith and culture. To have an open field for promoting its teaching, it opposed a theocratic society with the vision of a secularized, even atheistic one. This ideology brought it into conflict with a community which felt the descent of the Holy Spirit within history through the sacraments and the gifts of driving out evil spirits and healing the sick.

Instead of allowing themselves to become the prey of sects and sectarian evangelists, the Orthodox churches have made a certain number of missionary choices. Other orientations are of a pastoral nature, leaving priests free to draw their own conclusions as to appropriate Christian action. For example, all the churches have been challenged to take back the responsibility for the education of children and young people, including the training of catechists and teachers of religious studies in state schools. More and more faculties of theology, open to young women, are integrated into the structure of the university and subsidized by the state, thus offering the possibility of influencing the intellectual life of the country, as well as preparing candidates for the priesthood, teachers of religion and personnel for the social services.

Programmes to distribute the Bible, set up by lay associations and movements, have created close contacts with the churches of the Reformation traditions and evangelical communities. It is not surprising that during the WCC's seventh assembly (Canberra 1991), Orthodox participants and persons of the "evangelical" wing of the WCC spoke of a certain "rapprochement". Conversations have already begun with the conviction that "the evangelicals share several observations, questions and desires with the Orthodox churches and see the drawing closer of their positions as a challenge to break the divisions in Christianity".[8]

Another area for deepening cooperation is the relation of Christians to the economic and political structures in their countries. The Western practice is to address "non-theological factors" directly or in the framework of the "civil society". In the East we have too often allowed these forces to impose their directives and imperatives on society without adequate and authentic protest — perhaps out of a fear of being assimilated into the institutions which hold the reins of society.

We should not ignore the practical difficulties which may arise in setting up programmes to address the call to mission in Europe, specifically the risks of competitiveness and proselytizing. The advance of Roman Catholic missions in Orthodox countries is a case in point. The Orthodox have severely criticized the establishment of parallel ecclesiastical structures on their canonical territory without any consultation with them at all. It must be acknowledged that in the present psychological climate the Orthodox will inevitably begin with the assumption that any programme of evangelization "made in the West" is in fact a political programme and a tactic to expand the frontiers of the Roman Catholic Church. But ecumenism in these last years of the century must not consist in making more "separated brethren"!

The other aspect to be mentioned here is uniatism, which touches not only upon relations between the churches — whence the discouraging status quo in ecumenism — but also on relations with state governments.[9] From a political point of view it is certainly logical to restructure the network of uniate churches — those Christians who use the Byzantine rite but have been united to Rome since the late 16th century — to take back the places of worship and properties transferred to the Orthodox or confiscated by the state when they were banned by the communist regime. This is a question of repairing the injustice perpetrated against minorities and ethnic groups. In fact, in the name of law and justice for the uniate churches, a serious conflict has arisen with the Orthodox churches on the spot, taking violent form in the Western Ukraine, Slovakia and Romania. These episodes explain the popular anger against the violence of the uniates. For the ordinary people were the real victims of uniatism; only the hierarchy among the Orthodox accepted union with Rome, abandoning the faithful. The uniate church was a clerical one, whereas the people remained Orthodox at enormous risk.

The Orthodox documents on this matter[10] show clearly how geographical and missionary expansionism became a method in itself. The whole non-Catholic church became a target for uniatism as "the way to union", the only "bridge towards lost unity". While the "rite" of Orthodoxy is appreciated,[11] its doctrines have only secondary importance or are very debatable ones. Indeed, for the Bishop of Rome the unity would be a matter of a restoration of history, because all the Eastern churches were formerly faithful to the apostolic see of Rome.

NOTES

1. Cf. *On the Way to Fuller Koinonia*, report of Section II, p.239.

2. Cf. the report of the special assembly for Europe of the Roman Catholic bishops (Nov.-Dec. 1991), in *Service d'information*, no. 81, 1992, pp.112-57; and the apostolic exhortation *Christifideles Laici* (on the vocation and mission of the laity in church and world), Rome, Vatican Polyglot Press, 1988, pp.91-136.

3. Cf. "Unité des chrétiens et mission de l'Eglise", *Spiritus* (Paris), Vol. 23, no. 88, Sept. 1982, pp.293-300.

4. Cited in *Service d'information, loc. cit.*, p.65.

5. *Ibid.*, p.67.

6. "Lettre de la communauté monastique du Mont-Athos", *Episkepsis*, no. 465, 15 July 1991, p.3.

7. The phrase is taken from the Letter to the Bishops of the Catholic Church on Some Aspects of the Church's Understanding of Communion from the Congregation for the Doctrine of the Faith; English text in *L'Osservatore Romano*, no. 24, 17 June 1992.

8. Michael Kinnamon, ed., *Signs of the Spirit*, pp.279-86; cf. the report of the Orthodox-Evangelical consultation in Stuttgart (Feb. 1993) in *International Review of Mission*, Vol. 83, no. 331, 1994, pp.631-34.

9. Cf. Gennadios Limouris, *Aide-Mémoire on Uniatism*, Geneva, WCC, 1992. For the pastoral, practical and theological response to the problem of uniatism by the WCC central committee, following a series of team visits by the WCC and the Conference of European Churches and a consultation in July 1992, see *Minutes of the 44th Meeting of the WCC Central Committee*, Geneva, 1992, pp.158ff.

64 *The Liturgy after the Liturgy*

10. Cf. G. Lemopoulos, ed., *Your Will Be Done: Orthodoxy in Mission*, Geneva, WCC, 1989, p.51; "Message of the Primates of the Most Holy Orthodox Churches", Phanar, 1992, in Limouris, ed., *Orthodox Visions of Ecumenism*, pp.194ff.

11. Cf. *Rapport du colloque sur le renouveau dans la Liturgie orthodoxe*, Bucharest, Oct. 1991.

6. *The Spectrum of Orthodoxy*

The sudden liberation of the Orthodox churches in Central and Eastern Europe at the end of the 1980s and beginning of the 1990s has disclosed the extent to which the "Orthodox bloc", faithful to Eastern canonical order and tradition, is in fact a mosaic of nations, cultures, mentalities and social realities, held together by fragile alliances, threatened by unrevealed crises. Hidden realities, both positive and negative, now come to the surface: forces of resistance and endurance as well as compromise and collaboration.

The Orthodox have always made much of the fact that they did not pass through the divisions and schisms which have characterized the churches of the West. But they have endured a tragic period of atheistic political oppression. Accustomed to taking the conflicts and disasters of history for granted, Orthodox church historians may be tempted to minimize this period as a parenthesis within an overall continuity. But the experience and consequences of this historical break in the tradition cannot be ignored so easily.

What is the message of this period? How can oppression be transformed into liberation? The renewal of the Orthodox and of the ecumenical community at large depends on the answers. It is still too early to draw comprehensive lessons from such recent history: there is a mass of historical facts to be studied, and what is required is more than a mere descriptive analysis. Consequently, the situation of the Orthodox churches in post-communist Europe is already the object of varied and contradictory interpretations.

Mindful of their own role in the political antagonisms of the cold war, the churches themselves have been hesitant to undertake this historical analysis. The danger of not doing so arises from the eagerness of the new political and governmental leaders, beginning with Mikhail Gorbachev, to involve the churches in the moral reconstruction of society. Playing political games with the churches seems to be common to all systems, whether left or right, communist or capitalist. Some political leaders cover this cynical strategy with nationalistic demagoguery, while former communists now operate under the umbrella of religious ideology or humanism. This is why the churches must be clear about the meaning of their liberation for their life and mission.

New profiles and old stereotypes

Although recent attempts to express Orthodox conciliarity at the global level have demonstrated the complexity of the current situation of Orthodoxy and the difficulty of even identifying the critical questions on which the Orthodox churches must find common answers,[1] pressing questions like "What is Orthodoxy today?" and "What is Orthodoxy about?" cannot remain unanswered. The image of Orthodoxy, spoiled or eroded as it is, needs to be disclosed. Moral heresies covered up so as not to disturb the unity of the church during the time of oppression must now be brought to the surface. There is no sense in being enslaved by old historical and sociological analyses. What is the new profile of Orthodoxy in the light of the change in the countries of Central and Eastern Europe?

• To resist the destructive forces of the atheistic state, the Orthodox churches in communist countries relied on their traditional values — the liturgical assembly, the Christian family, the spirituality of prayer, popular piety, the witness of the martyrs. Living under oppression, they reduced their missionary role and their cultural influence. Now it must be asked how far Christian values and moral convictions were compromised by the totalitarian system. Were the churches at all able to formulate critical views in such political areas as human rights, religious liberty, economics? Without seeking to pass judgments, it must be acknowledged that the churches' political stance during this period makes it inevitable to raise such issues as the relationship of ecclesiology and politics and the church as a sociological community.

• The church in the world is fragile, weak and vulnerable, and its history is not a continuously upward evolution. Neither individual Christians, nor Christian communities, nor ecclesiastical institutions are immune from human failure, theological deviation, moral error. The church is a moral community, and its members' moral lapses may and often do threaten the credibility of its witness. To maintain the holiness of the church requires a constant moral struggle against many forms of evil. This recognition must shape our understanding of the mission of the church.

• Living in isolation, the Orthodox churches cultivated their identity in an exclusive and defensive way, and their ecclesiastical independence was exploited in the nationalistic interest of the communist states. Intimidated by the political agenda, the churches remained silent on most of the complicated and critical issues confronting society. Inevitably this created the impression that the Orthodox churches were several decades behind the times and indifferent to crises in the Christian community.

Often, indeed, they seemed to take these crises for granted, as though no serious effort moral engagement, much less repentance, were necessary.

• The Orthodox diaspora not only raises a canonical problem — the nature of their link to the mother churches — but also poses missionary and ecumenical issues. The rich and varied experiences of these churches has had little influence on the life of Orthodoxy as a whole. What does it mean to be "local" and "universal" in a diaspora situation? Orthodox conciliarity is seriously distorted by the failure to take seriously the emergence of new local churches. The universality of the Orthodox church is falsified by the impression that Orthodoxy is restricted to the historical churches.

• The Orthodox churches have been actively involved in the World Council of Churches from the beginning; and the WCC has actively assisted the Orthodox churches by helping to organize a long series of inter-Orthodox consultations, seminars and studies. In this "conciliar fellowship" a process of growing together, of deepening relations with other churches, has developed. The common search for visible unity has helped the Orthodox to appreciate the values of other Christian traditions, especially the ancient pre-Chalcedonian Eastern churches (Oriental Orthodox); and a wide range of theological convergence has been acknowledged.

• The slowness and delays in preparations for a great and holy synod of the Orthodox churches gives the impression that the Orthodox no longer trust universal projects and ecumenical councils. This attitude reinforces the scepticism of the faithful about the credibility of the ecclesiastical authorities. Failure to understand the new profile of the church, as Christians and as institution, falsifies the point of departure for the new situation. The churches still operate with general definitions and outdated symbols as though nothing had happened — though this is not to suggest that sociological analysis should replace a theological perception of history, for that would only mean falling into an ambiguous populist ideology.

Traces of a new martyrdom

During this century Christians in Central and Eastern Europe have endured one of the most brutal persecutions in history. The faithful, the priests and the bishops who were themselves victims of the tyrants cannot forget the memory of those who suffered for the faith of Christ and the hope of the church.

Humiliated and impoverished by the communist system, the Orthodox today lack the energy and resources to recollect these tragic experiences, to examine the stories, the documents, the testimonies — in a word, the history — of that period. Society as a whole seems to want to ignore that history and its implications for culture and spirituality. The only place to keep alive the memory of the new confessors is the liturgical congregation, where the faithful themselves ask the priest to pray for them. From time to time, the church leaders show the courage to commemorate the contemporary martyrs and saints.

In this way, the church can see how the life of the faithful is related to persecution, violence and death, how the eucharist is related to the cross and resurrection. In the space between heaven and hell, the Orthodox faithful carry in themselves the memory of this drama. Yet in the cherubim hymn they sing, "Now lay aside all earthly care". It is only redemption and forgiveness which can overcome the difficult memories; in fact, "none is worthy". As Jesus Christ descended to our very human condition, so suffering people have to descend to the hell of the tyrants and, marking the sign of the cross on the past, cry for them, "*Kyrie eleison*".

In many countries, Orthodoxy was associated with the imperial Byzantine dream of the "Christian East". In Russia, for example, the Slavophile movement cherishes exaggerated ambitions of Moscow as the "third Rome", holding sway over the whole Orthodox world — a vision which is not much different from the aspirations of Soviet political hegemony.

What remains after the loss by both Constantinianism and communism of their imperialistic possibilities is a lack of theological, intellectual and artistic creativity on the part of the "perestroika"-generation and the rise of all sorts of pseudo-religions and spiritualities, "false teachers" with "destructive opinions" who malign the way of truth (cf. 2 Pet. 2:1-3). Here a gigantic educational and spiritual effort is needed. But the demons of *homo sovieticus* have not been fully exorcised. Paralyzed by long decades of exclusion, the people approach democracy without passion, and many remain indifferent to dehumanizing powers and the needs and concerns of human beings.

But the most dramatic shift has taken place within the body of the church itself. To be sure, the gap between the church authorities and the faithful is nothing new. In old Russia, the authorities preferred an Orthodoxy which praised the nobility and dismissed the peasants as the "rest of the church". Even today there are those who believe that the political vision of Orthodoxy corresponds to aristocracy and monarchy.

Aggravating the gap between the leadership and the people has been the insensitivity to human and pastoral realities and social sins which largely excluded any criticism of the state-party domination and focused the attention of the hierarchy on institutional survival without real concern for the personal and social life or the culture of the faithful.

Another gap is opened up by those who take a fundamentalist view of the "true church" in which any talk of "renewal" of its life and mission is opposed on the ground that only by preserving the roots, the heritage, the identity of the indigenous church in an exclusive manner can revolution be avoided. Any innovations, they warn, would have the most dire consequences — whether it be adapting the liturgical calendar, replacing obsolete language in the liturgy and Bible translations, modernizing the hair styles and robes of the clergy, or opening the altar for the people and facing the congregation during the liturgy. Their absurd idea of "separating the sheep from the goats" here and now has also been coopted into a political coalition. These groups are proud of their intentionally polarizing attitude towards the "non-Orthodox" and their disregard for the ecumenical movement.

Distinctions to be made

The recent changes have liberated the Orthodox from exclusively abstract descriptions of their churches, uncovering the reality of their human qualities, contradictions and crises. This in turn has exposed contradictions that must be faced up to. For example, the solemn celebration of the liturgy in colourful vestments is an impressive moment of harmony and peace. But how does this *symbol* conveyed by the hierarchs relate to the concrete *reality* of their communities and their faithful? Compared with the splendour of their ceremonies, the actual situation of the priests and the congregations in many parts of the Orthodox fellowship is quite different.

To represent with humility what must be represented, the Orthodox need to draw on their heritage. To make the tradition alive, accessible and communicable in a credible way, complex and archaic structures perhaps need to be transformed. The point is not change for the sake of innovation, but to serve as an example for the renewal of society and its economic and political organization. Such renewal cannot be postponed on the pretext of preserving tradition or identity.

This is related to the place of the faithful in the church. While they are now free to take full responsibility for its life and mission, the churches are still hesitant to confront and debate the controversial imbalance between church authorities and the reality of the faithful laity.

It is an established historical fact that the political manifestations of communism appeared disproportionately in countries with predominantly Orthodox populations. The sociological and intellectual resistance to communism in these countries was easily annihilated, though the reasons for this differ from country to country. In Russia, the traditional spirituality of the humiliated Christ was not a strong preparation for the ideologies of the 20th century. In the Balkan countries the popular piety of *kenosis* developed during the 1930s put a great deal of emphasis on one's personal life and perfection but said little about political and social matters, so that the integration of personal life and social issues and the coherence between faith and social ethics were completely neglected.

This is reinforced by the fact that the Orthodox churches have not often spoken out publicly — for example, through encyclical letters — on social and economic matters, either to express a clear position or to offer guidance to the faithful.

Now, after years of avoiding what they have seen as the arena of worldly power struggles, the Orthodox churches have been called to an important role in the public life of countries struggling to build a state on the basis of democracy, justice and freedom. Social ethics and political involvement (in both declarations and actions) represent a new arena for Christian presence, requiring careful orientation; and before learning the principles of political diakonia and shaping a civil society, they are preoccupied with preventing the return of the ancient demons of totalitarianism.

The risks accompanying the presence of the church in public life in "post-secularized" society should not be underestimated. In taking a stand on public issues, ambiguities are inevitable; yet the church has to live out its peculiar sacramental identity as a sign of the kingdom and a provisional pilgrim community on the way to the kingdom. Religion and politics cannot be separated: to the extent that each is searching for a moral community they need each other. But there is a difference between the essence of the church and the nature of society. Politics is never a system of salvation, because of the ambiguous nature of power.[2]

There is a movement towards new local autocephalous churches, in recognition of their particular languages and indigenous leadership, and towards national ecclesiastical authority as a rejection of submission to what have been seen as the historical centres (the "mother churches"). Orthodox churches in most of the countries which have recently recovered their national independence — Ukraine, Moldavia, Estonia, Latvia, Macedonia, Albania — have claimed full autonomy and autocephaly.

At the same time there is a deep sensitivity to the reality of the church universal. The concept of the local church, based on the idea of the canonical territory of a particular nation, identifiable through its culture and language, had privileged the autonomy and freedom of the people of God in a specific place. But ecclesiastical autonomy, while a source of freedom and solidarity for the nation, is no guarantee of freedom from nationalistic captivity. So today in Eastern Europe, where the majority of the Orthodox are located, we see the moral authority of the primates being disputed by their own people. They have been unable to cope with the rise of nationalism, ethnic divisions and even civil wars or influence the political and social scene.

The failure of nations to be reconciled with other nations in the same Orthodox country signals the crucial need for a sense of the fulness of koinonia in the church universal in order to manifest the catholicity of local churches. Orthodox faith is not only an element in the building of nations; it has a catholic dimension as well. It is not "Oriental" or "Occidental", not "Latin" or "Greek", but evangelical, though it is experienced in various ways by different nations and cultures. If the autonomy of the local church becomes a liberating force within the church universal, the Orthodox may also regain the place which was once theirs in the ecumenical community due to the great influence of certain personalities.

The primary ground for the Orthodox opposition to Western missionaries is ecclesiological. The Orthodox refuse to become a *terra missionis* of the Western churches. The universalistic view of the church (among Roman Catholics) and the individualistic idea of salvation (among Protestants) have overshadowed the idea of the church as communion; and the most destructive attack on this understanding came from the theory and practice of mission by Western churches, both Catholic and Protestant, in the 19th century: the expansion of power and influence of Western churches and missionary societies into new territories, and the resulting devaluation and disintegration of indigenous local groups.

While trends and developments in missiology today no longer fit this description, new dangers — sectarian and ethnic interests, secular and

Christian nationalisms, religious conflicts — menace the church as an ecumenical communion.

Reformulating the terms of Orthodoxy

The language of communication. To speak about Orthodoxy effectively requires a discipline of communication which will on the one hand enable the sharing of Orthodox tradition and teaching in and beyond Orthodox contexts (the sense of universality) and on the other hand recognize diversity and avoid uniformity. Too often, when the Orthodox speak about themselves in an ecumenical context, they do so in a defensive way, so that nobody listens to them. Orthodox history and present experience are ignored sometimes because of the reticence of the Orthodox, sometimes because there are too many repetitions and generalities, which leave the impression that the Orthodox operate mainly with ecclesiastical slogans, sometimes because they overemphasize historical references to the early origins of Orthodoxy, as if it had no biblical roots.

As a WCC consultation some years ago put it, "we have to see to what extent traditional church language, both verbal and visual, has in many parts of both Western and Eastern Europe become esoteric, the language of insiders. In this situation, it is the duty of the church to take seriously the rapid changes in thinking and sensibility that are taking place in what they may regard, with some detachment, as the secular world."[3]

The methodological problem is that in the ecumenical dialogue the Orthodox may use Western theological and philosophical concepts and symbols which are common in ecumenical discourse — the Constantinian era, the "end of history", the disappearance of the *Volkskirche*, "religionless Christianity", secular humanism, the "two kingdoms" — which are not current in the East. The question is how the language of the Eastern churches expresses the same realities in a way that is relevant to others.

The Orthodox tradition relies a great deal on images, signs and symbols, not only to communicate the gospel but also to denounce the dark forces that disfigure creation instead of revealing the beauty and victory of the kingdom present and to come. Facing the destructive and dangerous function which pictures often have in the modern world, contemporary iconography, pointing to God's capacity for changing the old into the new, for lifting a fallen world to God's glory, can provide a new vision of history and understanding of creation. By bearing the hope of one day seeing the whole creation becoming Christlike and perfectly transparent to the glory of God (Rom. 8:18,30), this art may participate in the transformation of creation.

A people of the church. The Orthodox are privileged to have a people of faith with a strong memory and attachment to the tradition. This quality has to be seen from two perspectives: on the one hand, because of apostolic continuity and patristic faithfulness, the church cannot elude the tradition, whose permanent teaching is important for the continuity of the people; on the other hand, people of the present are needed to carry the tradition.

As evidence surfaces of the decay in many of the institutions and doctrines around which the Orthodox fellowship was built, the people ask why all this has been kept from them. Moreover, lay movements and groups want to express themselves and to shape "civil society" without the limitations ecclesiastical authorities often impose. What can be expected from official statements on public and moral affairs which are heavy, authoritarian and insensitive and do not reflect a conciliar spirit? Old canonical prescriptions need a fresh reception for new credibility. Therefore, the institutional church must be receptive to the renewing force of the Holy Spirit, who is able to reach out to the entire *oikoumene*. The Spirit appears in "tongues of fire" (Acts 2:3) because the Spirit brings a power which, like fire, dares all things. The Spirit will empower a new generation with forces of renewal and prophetic vision: "In the last days it will be, God declares, that I will pour out my Spirit upon all flesh, and your sons and your daughters shall prophesy, and your young men shall see visions, and your old men shall dream dreams" (Acts 2:17).

An ecclesiology of catholicity. For Orthodox ecclesiology, the church is more than a community with a special vocation. It is the sign of the contemporary presence of Christ and active compassion in God's world. Against all instrumental and operational views of the church, Orthodox theology insists clearly that the communion of the Holy Trinity is the very foundation of ecclesial communion. The trinitarian divine koinonia generates and shapes communion in the body of Christ. The all-encompassing will of God sustains the catholicity of the church. The church glorifies the three persons of the Trinity as the unity of God. A deficient theology of this divine koinonia will have consequences for the understanding of ecclesial communion.

The primary point of the ecumenical movement is not undoing historical wrongs but manifesting in history the mystery of God. In his meditation on his communion with the Father (John 17:20-24), Jesus' prayer is that all may be one as he and his Father are one. This is not a semantic analogy but the affirmation of interconnected ontological realities. The divine communion determines the quality of the human community. The concern of Jesus for all and for the unity of all is part of his historical experience. "What we have seen and heard we declare to you, so that you and we together may share in a common life, that life which we share with the Father and his Son Jesus Christ" (1 John 1:3). John sees the community of the Holy Trinity as a reality which holds together human society and orders common life. The new life is life within community.

Liturgical identity. As we have seen throughout this book, the Orthodox not only integrate liturgy into their piety, but also make it a vital element of their life and faith, going beyond the boundaries of Christian worship to serve the missionary and diaconal community at large. For liturgy is not an escape into interior issues of personal ethics and piety, a turning away from evangelism and social ethics. Liturgy is an area in which the church can say and do something for the new society. Its energies should serve human history and the human condition. Orthodoxy provides not a theory of history but a therapy for the human community. But the most important dimension of liturgy is that it provides a mechanism for the Christian community to be not only *in* but also *beyond* the culture, to be an *inclusive* rather than an *exclusive* fellowship.

To proclaim and celebrate the faith means to seek the rights of the nations and of national minorities, to protect the differences in culture and language, to ensure the participation of women, to struggle for an inclusive community and against racism and xenophobia. There is an ecumenism of the poor, economically and intellectually, whether they are in the church or outsiders in relation to the church. There is an ecumenism of women, who ask that their spirituality, dignity and competence be recognized.

Capacity for reception and recognition. Orthodoxy has always had a special place among other forms of historic Christianity. Generally it is categorized as a particular Eastern tradition, distinctive and different from all others. This static juxtaposition of confessional entities needs to give way to a constructive confrontation between Christian traditions and cultures. This would show that Roman Catholicism and Protestantism are not the "owners" of European Christianity, but just churches which have specific vocations and missions. Then we need to explore *oikonomia* as an active working principle and a way of understanding diversity in unity.

Orthodox theology has a special concern for the total *oikonomia* of the Holy Spirit, who dwells in the church in a specific way but works in many other realms, being the Spirit of "all flesh". The current understanding of secularization in Europe is that of an area in which the Spirit, who appears in tongues of fire, does not dare to operate. If the Holy Spirit is at work in that secular world, we should be open to the manifestations of this, no matter how unlikely the forms or the places in which they may appear. The fear of fundamentalists that we will thus devalue the identity of the Christian community must be challenged on the grounds of the biblical call for openness to all, an invitation to break barriers (cf. Luke 14:21-24; Matt. 22:1-4).

The viability and relevance of Orthodoxy are closely tied to how its canonical unity is structurally expressed at the local and global levels. Conciliarity at the local level has constituted the heart of the renewal process, and broad conciliarity has been the vital link among the churches. Today, however, conciliarity at the global level especially has shown signs of brokenness and weakness. This is reflected in the debate about the pan-Orthodox identity of the Ecumenical Patriarchate and its jurisdiction over the 20 million Orthodox in the diaspora. For example, the Ecumenical Patriarchate took more than a half century to solve the "Bulgarian schism" (1872 to 1945) and deferred for many years the recognition of the autocephaly of the churches in Georgia, Poland, Czechoslovakia and Finland. The Moscow Patriarchate quickly declared new autocephalous churches in Japan and the USA, but has delayed giving the same status in the Ukraine and Moldavia. Similar tensions of this kind are the split of the church in Macedonia from the canonical link with Serbia since 1967 and the current schism in the church in Bulgaria.

The Orthodox churches must respond together in a new way to their vocation, considering the emergence of a new people of God with their new experience and vision of history, recent growth and theological achievements as the background for all new developments. This quality of Orthodoxy will open new ways not only to be present in the European context but also on the ecumenical scene.

The ecumenical reputation of Orthodoxy lies in its unbroken faithfulness to the apostolic tradition, to the undivided church, in other words, in its sense of catholicity. Yet it is presented as one historical form of Christianity, alongside Roman Catholicism and Protestantism, having its "confessional" identity fixed in a certain era of church history. Here we need clarification and differentiation. If Orthodoxy is the *ecumenical* (that is, non-confessional, non-denominational) form of church tradition, what conclusions can be drawn from this? Does this provide sufficient ground for taking as comprehensive as possible a view of various confessional traditions? Is Orthodoxy concerned with other "kinds" of ecclesiology? Can we continue to declare that the Orthodox firmly reject "equality of the confessions"?[4]

The integrity of Orthodoxy
The sense of praise and beauty. One of the most impressive elements in Orthodox spirituality is the impulse of the faithful of all categories and ages to be totally involved in the action of the liturgy as a feast, the desire to see, to enter into the holy place, to concelebrate and to take holy communion. Liturgy is not a matter of time, but of moving towards the glorious high throne to praise the presence of God. In this physical movement towards the altar it is impossible to be uninvolved or to remain motionless. Here is a unique spirit of conviviality and collective pilgrimage in a space which symbolizes the beauty of God. People need to rediscover the beautiful sacred nature of their life and milieu. This is not simply a matter of popular religiosity perpetuating humble piety. It is the biblical understanding of the church as a priestly people standing before God, an inexhaustible people who are receiving divine resources. Often people place food and drink in the middle of the church to be blessed by the priest — food for pilgrims.

No dichotomy between person and community. The notion of "neighbour" is essential for the definition of a Christian. The liturgy opens the way to the neighbour as a person through whom our salvation is possible. It does not allow the religious hypocrisy which claims to honour God while bypassing the neighbour, for God loves all people: "I was daily his delight, rejoicing before him always, rejoicing in his inhabited world and delighting in the human race" (Prov. 8:30f.).

St John Chrysostom speaks about the two altars, one in the temple, the other in the public square, where Christians offered their gifts. He denounces a spirituality which has no social implications, which closes its eyes to the evils in society. The essential is not to choose between the two, but to celebrate both. It is clear that Christians in Eastern Europe after the communist period have a lot of room for social diakonia. This diakonia can become a healing instrument for society at large. One can see families who, after the communion at the liturgy, call together their friends and neighbours (Luke 15:6) and share their food and drink with them. As they receive the communion from one bread and chalice, so they also have to share their bread with those in need.

The "catholic" dimension of salvation. The doctrine of the Holy Spirit is central for understanding not only the nature and unity of the church, local and universal, but also the totality of God's saving action in history and in creation. The question of how God's work in history and the church's mission in history are related is an old one. What is new in recent ecumenical discussion is the concern for the total *oikonomia* of the Holy Spirit, who dwells in the church in a specific way but works in many other realms as well. The point here is not so much the distinctive mode of presence of the Spirit within and outside the church, but our conception of God's purpose in the diversity of this presence. The interpretation of the *oikonomia* of the Holy Spirit should be liberated from ecclesiastical territorial limits because the Holy Spirit acts in the church precisely in order to reach the entire *oikoumene*, God's temple.

In the Pentecost event God constituted his new people, built on the incarnation, death and resurrection of Jesus Christ, who bestowed on them peace and the Holy Spirit, entrusted to them the care of the whole world and sent them as pastors all over the earth. But the church established at Pentecost is not a sect or an exclusive community. Jesus refused to consider his community as a closed group. When the disciples told him that they had tried to stop someone who was casting out demons in Jesus' name, he told them, "Do not stop him, for no one who does a deed of power in my name will be able soon afterward to speak evil of me" (Mark 9:38-40).

Not only the "catholicity" of salvation and the universality of the church but also the orientation of history are within the hands of the Spirit, as is testified at Pentecost. The influence of the Spirit cannot be limited to the canonical territory of the church; it is not a matter of jurisdiction or geographical extension. The problem is not to measure the universality of the church but to recognize that the Spirit has a project and a realm which go beyond the institutional sphere of the church. The church itself is called to proclaim that God reveals himself and acts "in many and various ways" (Heb. 1:1) in the power of the Holy Spirit and that while the church is a peculiar sacramental instrument within the entire *oikonomia* of the Spirit, God's community embraces all who are on the way, whom we should not stop even if they do not follow us. Therefore the ecumenical fellowship exists not only to repair history, to compare the situations of churches, to register doctrines of common reference, to count up the attempts for unions, and to monitor the contacts, dialogues, frustrations and contradictions. It exists to keep alive the sense of the global history of salvation and the biblical memory of being rooted in God's covenant with all humanity and all creation.

All baptized into one body. The mutual recognition of baptism among the member churches of the WCC has missionary, spiritual and pastoral implications. For example, we saw earlier how it is related to the problem of proselytism. But the recognition of baptism is not only an evangelical-Orthodox problem. Indeed, many Orthodox are not ready to recognize as valid a baptism outside the sacramental order and ministry of the church and many evangelicals do not recognize the form of baptism practised by the Orthodox. Beyond that, however, lies a fundamental question of Christian identity: what is the meaning of baptism in relation to the identity of the disciples of Christ and members of his body? What is the role of baptism in creating the communion of the faithful, in becoming through the same Spirit sisters and brothers of one another? What is the *relational* dimension of baptism?

In trying to explain how the life of Christ takes form in the life of the Christian, St Paul attached great importance to baptism (Rom. 6:3-11), the sacrament in which we receive the total condition of Christ in our human condition. "You have clothed yourself with Christ" (Gal. 3:27). Through baptism we are "planted together with Christ"; we enter into the very essence of his death and life; we are rooted in him. This is an experience that takes us to a reality beyond ourselves, yet becomes our new identity. Paul said that we will never know how God's life is drawn into our life. We do not understand completely this sacramental passover, but we know that being buried with him in baptism, we will be raised with him.

Baptism does not merely set us free from sin, but also confers a condition opposite to sin, that is, holiness. Christians become a new creation, heirs of the new life, which is the power of the world to come (Heb. 6:5). The very identity of the faithful is realized and confirmed in baptism.

We share Christ's condition in baptism, because he himself shared our condition in his incarnation. We share his Spirit because he took our human flesh. And precisely the one Spirit we received in baptism creates one body of many members: "For in the one Spirit we are all baptized into one body — Jews and Greeks, slaves or free — and we were all made to drink of one Spirit" (1 Cor. 12:13). One Spirit, one body: the body of Christ. Not only are we all together members of the body, but we are also members of each other. Not only does Christ as head secure the unity of the body, but also the Spirit strengthens the articulations of the body.

Baptism means surrendering the old image of individual existence to a new mode of existence by incorporation into a communion. In his mystery, God has chosen us to be his people and to save us as a people. We discover our identity as members of the body of Christ in our relationship with other members. Recognition of baptism means believing in the power of God, giving the identity of the Christian and forming a Christian community, changing the old into new, transforming the ancient world into a new creation.

Teaching ministry and critical sense. "In our church it is the people who are the defenders of truth." This famous phrase from the encyclical of the Eastern patriarchs of 1848 encapsulates a sound tradition regarding the charismatic capacity of the whole body of the church to discern the truth. This encyclical was published in the context of a controversy over the practice of the Latin church to promulgate doctrines of faith as dogmas without the explicit consensus of the church. While recognizing the bishops' teaching authority, the encyclical insisted that the exercise of this authority is inseparable from the teaching ministry of the faithful. It may appear as democratic ecclesiology, but the practice has a profound biblical basis, and history offers extensive evidence of the experience of the people in defending the Orthodox faith.

The Orthodox need to renew this tradition in order to return the sense of being a community of faith to the parish, to reactivate the teaching obligation of the priest and the influence of the theologians on public opinion. Those responsibilities have been neglected in recent times in favour of a theology based on the experience and meditation of ascetic writers and mystical fathers. This authentically Orthodox school of mystical, noetic knowledge preserves the sense of mystery and holiness. God is a reality never defined and never verifiable. Even in revelation God protects his mystery. The teaching ministry in this perspective belongs supremely to those who reach a degree of illumination and sanctification by inner prayer and ascetic life.

But the ethos of Orthodoxy as a disciplined community has been shaped by the public preaching and teaching of those who have not only been great biblical scholars and preachers but also ministers of the edification of the church. The "patristic" church is known in history for its passion for oratory, for the ministry of the word. Homiletics and catechetics deeply influenced the mind of the Orthodox people. Even though St John Chrysostom criticized the infatuation of Christians with oratory, he was convinced that the best pastoral instrument is teaching by word of mouth. He believed in the healing power of the word of God: preaching is not a matter of simple eloquence and speech in order to gain popularity, but a matter of the search for truth.

Today the teaching ministry must be renewed in three directions:
— The people should understand every aspect of doctrine and not be allowed to remain ignorant on the theory that they are unable to examine the profundity of faith. To "teach" without explaining what is being taught is to disregard the congregation, whereas to preach with passion and enthusiasm, with "grace seasoned with salt" (Col. 4:6), creates a climate in which the health of the community is secured.
— The people need more clarity and intelligence of the faith in order to be ready to give account of the hope which is in them (1 Pet. 3:15). In the face of unsound teachings, heresies and doctrinal conflicts, it is the responsibility of the faithful to correct those who are stumbling with persuasiveness and conviction.
— The people would like to participate in the incarnation of the word of God in human history, to see the transforming power of the gospel in society, to experience the therapy of the word of God. This is not the mystical way of theology — whatever values that may have — but a theology which teaches the history of humanity as it was incarnated in the life and ministry of Jesus Christ, history which enters the life of a particular community.

The power of consensus. The Orthodox understand their witness as a contemporary symbol of the fact that visible ecclesial communion has been possible in the history of the church around the fundamentals of Christian faith, ethics and practice, expressed for example in the Nicene-Constantinopolitan Creed of 381. This communion has not been perfect, but it has been a witness of a new reality in the world, without which the world has no meaning, a force of unity preventing the churches from being locked into situations of ultimate division.

In spite of the conflictual and divisive history of the degradation of historic Christianity, the local churches did succeed in having a common mind, in articulating together a common confession of faith, in making decisions as one body with many members. There was a time of conciliarity at the ecumenical level, objective, concrete, having as its core the tradition, the transmitted apostolic heritage, including holy scripture. It was historically possible to confess, "We believe in one holy, catholic and apostolic church". The Orthodox claim to stand for this tradition. Therefore, Orthodox participation is extremely important in the ecumenical exercise of discovering similarities and differences not only among the member churches of the World Council of Churches but also between the WCC and the Roman Catholic Church.

As the Orthodox always say, irreconcilable doctrinal differences undermine the very foundation of the unity of the church. The positive theological convergence reflected in *Baptism, Eucharist and Ministry* (1982) is thus ecumenically important as a sign that in their effort to restore the visible unity of the church universal the churches take seriously the common doctrine of faith, and that the issues of baptism, eucharist and ministry are central to the faith and teaching of the church. BEM has brought the doctrines of faith and theological matters into the centre of ecumenical reflection and debate.

BEM indicates that the churches decided to speak together at a particular moment on their ecumenical pilgrimage. Behind the document approved in Lima lies a good deal of ecumenical experience and discussion. It is not an abstract reconstruction or combination of ecumenical ideas, but an attempt to write a theological text with an ecumenical character and to avoid a merely confessional approach. Here lies both the value and the problem of the document.

In its search for the visible unity of the church, the WCC is of course vitally concerned with mission and unity at the local congregational level. But it has to cope with the church as a universal body. Yet it cannot produce an ecumenical statement in a normative way. Nor is there any easy way to regulate the diversity within the church universal: the differences of emphasis and terminology, the variety of schools and perceptions of theology, the multiplicity of cultures. Differences of emphasis are repeatedly elevated in degree into conflicts of principle. Therefore, before analyzing the BEM document chapter by chapter, we must answer a general question: what concept and image of unity does the whole text convey? BEM may accentuate one or another tradition or respond to specific contemporary subjects, but essentially it intends to emphasize the authority and contemporary relevance of the common traditions of the church universal, not by isolating a body of abstract principles and concepts, but by affirming the essentials of faith around which ecumenical practice takes place today.

Ascesis: a spirituality of detachment. With their "sacramental" understanding of Christian life and the church, the Orthodox are very keen on models of Christian spirituality for every time: how people experience and manifest their faith. The church as body of Christ and temple of the Holy Spirit is not to be a mirror of society, but a challenging reality and symbol for it. While living in the midst of history, the church needs an attitude of repentance and humility so that it can draw away from sinful complicity with the world. The church is "holy" because it is linked to the event of Pentecost, when the Holy Spirit called koinonia to be a prophetic sign and sacrament of the kingdom of God in history.

To this we may add the existential sense of *martyria*, of the suffering cross, which is very vivid to the Orthodox. It is the promise of the gospel that the only people who are guaranteed the synergy of the Holy Spirit are those who proclaim the truth before the powers of this world (cf. Luke 12:8-12).

NOTES

1. Cf., e.g., the "Message of the Primates of the Holy Orthodox Churches" (1992) in Limouris, ed., *Orthodox Visions of Ecumenism, loc. cit.* For a general profile of Orthodoxy see Kallistos Ware, "Eastern Christendom", in John McManners, ed., *History of Christianity*, Oxford and New York, Oxford UP, 1992, pp.123-62; Evi Voulgaraki-Pissina, "Aspects of Orthodox Church Life in the Balkans", in *Remembering the Future: The Challenge of the Churches in Europe*, New York, Friendship Press, 1995, pp.87-98.

2. Cf. Jan-Milic Lochman, *Reconciliation and Liberation*, Belfast, Christian Journals Ltd, 1980, p.16.

3. *Come and See: Renewal Through Iconography*, Geneva, WCC, 1988, pp.6f.

4. Cf. the statement by the third preconciliar pan-Orthodox conference (Chambésy, 1986): "The Orthodox Church, faithful to her ecclesiology, to the identity of her internal structure and to the teaching of the undivided church, while participating in the WCC, does not accept the idea of the 'equality of confessions' and cannot consider church unity as an interconfessional adjustment. In this spirit, the unity which is sought within the WCC cannot simply be the product of theological agreements alone. God calls every Christian to the unity of faith which is lived in the sacrament and the tradition, as experienced in the Orthodox Church" (text of the report in Limouris, *Orthodox Visions of Ecumenism*, pp.112ff.).

7. The Dynamics of Liturgy in Mission

In discussing the missionary nature of the church, the Orthodox have proposed a typology of mission and witness which corresponds to the history of their own mission — and in particular to the consistent tradition in which worship and liturgy have been an essential element in proclaiming and confessing Christ. We have called this typology the liturgy after the liturgy.

Ecumenical echoes
The theme of the "liturgy after the liturgy" has been taken up in numerous recent ecumenical theological discussions, and not only by Orthodox theologians. While an exhaustive catalogue of these is beyond the purposes of this book, it may be helpful to cite a few examples of how this theme is being developed to illuminate various critical concerns in the churches and the ecumenical movement today.

A case in point is the recent ecumenical discussion of ecclesiology and ethics, with its far-reaching implications for how the role of the church as a community in which the faithful are morally formed bears on the quest for the unity of the church and its mission in the world. Reformed theologian Lewis Mudge identifies a number of models according to which the church-world relationship has been addressed, including what he calls the "sacramental model". This model, he says,

> sees the very substance of the world's work, with the values embodied in its practices, taken up and transformed in the eucharistic act under the forms of bread, wine and the presence of the gathered community. We incorporate the "liturgy beyond the liturgy" into the liturgy itself and vice-versa. We reorder the very substance of our practical interactions with society and with creation into a new and transformative story, one which changes their substance to become the expression of Christ's presence among us in the power of the Holy Spirit.[1]

The relation between eucharist and the creation, another key theme in contemporary ecumenical discussion, has been emphasized by Nicholas K. Apostola:

> In the Orthodox understanding of the eucharist, when the bread and wine are offered to God they stand as signs for the creation (i.e., wheat and grapes) that

God entrusted to us, now transformed by human labour. God takes our gift, the offering back of the creation which he made, and sends down upon us a greater gift: the body and blood of his Son. We have grace upon grace (John 1:16), and grow from glory to glory (2 Cor. 3:18). In the act of worship, God transforms all those things that he has given us into a more beautiful reality than we could have ever imagined possible.[2]

George Guiver points out how the twofold movement of the "saving mysteries" reflected in the liturgy also has implications for our relations with our neighbours:

> One way in which the saving events are present in the liturgy is through their real presence in us, in our lives, in the lives of our neighbours and in the daily "liturgy" of living in, through and among them. We bring the presence *with* us when we come to church. These eternal themes of the drama of life want to reach out to the transcendent, to transcend themselves (this is God himself with creation, his Spirit within us, crying, "Abba!"). We naturally gather this up by coming together as the Body of Christ, and God again produces exactly the same things, the saving mysteries, but travelling in the opposite direction, from the transcendent descending towards us, as we in the liturgy make the ascent to his kingdom. God reaches out towards himself in us, and the two movements come together in the marriage-feast of the Lamb.
>
> There are in fact two dimensions to the same thing: Christ in our neighbour, and Christ in the liturgy. The former merely pursued on its own (as is often the case in the West) leads to spiritual exhaustion, while the latter pursued in isolation can cause God to withdraw, so that we are in danger of being left with an empty shell.[3]

From an African Orthodox perspective, Bishop Jonah Lwanga points to the outworking of Christian fellowship in what he calls "meta-liturgical life":

> In the *meta-eucharistic life* of Orthodox Africans... there are some characteristics of cultural activities related to the phenomenon of *agape* (fellowship) of the church of Corinth (1 Cor. 11:20-34). Specifically, we can see the emotional activities like excitement, chanting, dancing and, eventually, getting a common meal together. These activities... have the purpose of more affection, fellowship and association of members. They are activities of a festive character in the bond of love, the church body. Therefore, to understand these activities of Africans fully, after the holy eucharist, the sense of agape must be considered. Although in this context of Africa the idea of fellowship presupposes almost opposite situations and conditions from those reproved by the apostle Paul in Corinth.[4]

"Sharing" with neighbours in need was a key principle in the social thought of the church fathers:

> Eucharistic communion means nothing without human and social sharing, without identification with those people who, through most of their existence, go poor, hungry and naked: "The bread that remains uneaten in your house is the bread of the hungry. The tunic hanging in your wardrobe is the tunic of the naked. The footwear that remains unused in your house is that of the poor who go barefoot. The money that you keep buried away is the money of the poor. You can tell how many injustices you commit by counting the benefits you could bestow" (St Basil, Homily 4, on Luke 12:18).
>
> The human and social issues constitute in fact an integral part of the pastoral commitment of the church, and Orthodoxy cannot ignore today the fact that people inside and outside the church are looking for a new humanity and for a new social order. We are living an entirely new social situation in which the church needs to think afresh about the coherence between the spiritual realities of the Christian faith and the structures of the surrounding society. History and the experience of the saints have much to teach us.[5]

Boris Bobrinskoy places the idea of the liturgy after the liturgy in terms of the fundamental spiritual principle reflected in the rhythm of Sundays and weekdays:

> The sending forth of the faithful at the end of the liturgy has a profound symbolic and sacramental significance. The "*ite, missa est*" of the Roman mass or the "let us go in peace" of the Byzantine liturgies, this "sending out" of the faithful, is only the announcement of the end of the first stage of the eucharist... What follows is not so much an "exit" from the church as an "entrance" by the church into the world, continuing the sending forth of the disciples by the risen Lord (Matt. 28:18-20; Mark 16:15-20) in the power of the Spirit of Pentecost. When we leave the church, we enter another mode of the liturgy which is the "liturgy after the liturgy". This is the passage from Sunday, the day of the Lord, to the week.
>
> Sunday would have no meaning if it were not the first of seven days and at the same time the eighth, that is the fullness. The entire week then signifies preparation for Sunday, and the pitch of this waiting increases the closer Sunday comes. Then, when we leave the church, it is a fullness of life in Christ that we take with us into the world for the entire week. Consequently, the alternation of Sunday and the week is a fundamental spiritual principle and the very meaning of the liturgy.[6]

The impact of the liturgy on Christian mission, culture and political discipline has been underlined by many other theologians, Orthodox and others alike.[7] Here we may conclude with some eloquent words from Theodore Stylianopoulos:

> The fire of Christ's love is experienced and shared in a continuous movement of gathering as the faithful and going out to others. The gathering of the community of faith occurs supremely in corporate acts of prayer and worship, especially the eucharist, the central mystery of the presence of Christ, which nourishes, renews and empowers the entire life of the church. But the eucharist is offered for the life of the world; it cannot be separated from life, and therefore necessarily leads to a "liturgy after the liturgy" — a mission to the world in diverse ministries and various forms.[8]

To gather the church

To summarize, the main affirmations of the typology of the liturgy after the liturgy are the following:

— Mission cannot be exercised without reference to the church as a community contemporary with Christ. The mission of the church is not to build up the kingdom of God out of historical forces and materials, but to announce and show the kingdom in the eucharistic assembly as a symbol of the final recapitulation of all creation and all nations.

— At the heart of the doctrine of the church is faith in the triune God, rooted in the scriptures and in the testimony of the apostles who proclaimed the gospel of Jesus Christ. That faith is the content of a personal confession without which there is neither baptism nor eucharist. Where that faith is distorted, repentance and correction are necessary, because the koinonia of the triune God is the paradigm of the church as koinonia.

— Proclaiming Christ through liturgy implies the inculturation of worship and preaching in a language which can be understood. The link between one gospel and the diverse cultures of our world is a positive reality to be maintained, but not at the expense of breaking the links which unite everyone to each other.

— In the liturgy the proclamation of the gospel is not disconnected from the communion, because there is no dichotomy between the ministry and teaching of Christ and his death, resurrection and reconciliation.

— The whole communion of saints is gathered at the liturgy.

— To respond to the missionary and pastoral needs of the faithful, each local church has the responsibility to modify, expand and propose new

"liturgies" and new forms of "diakonia" after the eucharistic liturgy, thus showing a liturgical attitude in all areas of human life.
— There is a liturgy after the liturgy because Christians pursue their witness and vocation outside the temple, in the street, in social halls, in the wider society. Nourished by the eucharist, the pilgrim bread,[9] the food for missionaries and evangelists, Christians are sent out — "Go forth in peace, in the name of the Lord" — to witness in faithful discipleship in the common round of daily life. Their authority flows from their liturgical sending, which becomes fruitful through personal authenticity.

All these elements are needed if Christ's witness is to be complete. The typology of mission as liturgy after the liturgy can help us to understand the connections among the various forms and definitions of mission: as proclamation and invitation emphasizing personal salvation, as response to God's merciful will for the whole of humanity, as actions of service aimed at the transformation of society, as witness to God's justice and righteousness against inhuman conditions and unjust social structures, as a means for personal discipleship and holiness, as pastoral care responding to God's compassion for lost humanity.

Orthodox spirituality should be unfolded not only in sumptuous but often empty cathedrals, not only in rich ceremonial services, but also in the midst of the people. Orthodoxy needs more people like Mother Sofia, who died in 1996: people who go outside the temple, as she did in celebrating daily the "liturgy after the liturgy" in the streets of Lausanne, among the poor, the marginalized, the homeless, the refugees, the strangers of contemporary cities. In so doing she became a symbol of God's compassion for suffering humanity in any time and in every place.

The liturgy after the liturgy is an inspiration and impulse for reconstructing the church in history after the eucharistic model and vision. In the words of a prayer from the *Didache* (second century): "As this broken bread was scattered upon the mountains, and being gathered together became one, so may your church be gathered together from the ends of the earth into your kingdom; for yours is the glory and the power, through Jesus Christ, for ever and ever."

NOTES

1. Lewis S. Mudge, "Ecclesiology and Ethics in Current Ecumenical Debate", *The Ecumenical Review*, Vol. 48, no. 1, 1996, p.20; cf. David J. Bosch, *Dynamique de la mission chrétienne: Histoire et avenir des modèles missionnaires*, Geneva, Labor et Fides, 1995, pp.276f., 691.

2. Nicholas K. Apostola, "Theology as Doxology", *Ministerial Formation*, no. 657, Oct. 1994, p.45.

3. George Guiver, "Between East and West: Odo Casel and the Liturgical Mystery", in Ioan Ica, ed., *Person and Communion: Homage to Fr Dumitru Staniloae*, Sibiu, 1993, p.308.

4. J. Lwanga, "Cultural Expressions of the Younger African Orthodox Churches" (unpublished paper from the consultation of WCC Orthodox member churches on "The Gospel in Diverse Cultures", Addis Ababa, Jan. 1996).

5. Ion Bria, "Renewal of the Tradition through Pastoral Witness", *International Review of Mission*, Vol. 65, no. 258, 1976, p.185.

6. Boris Bobrinskoy, "Prière du coeur et eucharistie", in Ioan I. Ica, ed., *op. cit.*, pp.631f.

7. Cf., e.g., Olivier Clément, *La révolte de l'Esprit*, Paris, Stock, 1979, p.106; M. A. Costa de Beauregard, *L'Orthodoxie*, Paris, Buchet-Chastel, 1979, pp.124-26; Christos Yannaras, *La liberté de la morale*, Genève, Labor et Fides, 1982, p.199; Emilianos Timiadis, *Priest, Parish, Renewal*, Brookline MA, Holy Cross Orthodox Press, 1994, pp.116f.; René Marichal, "La Mission orthodoxe dans le monde contemporain", *Spiritus*, no. 139, May 1995, p.199; James J. Stamoulis, "The Imperative of Mission in Orthodox Theology", *Orthodoxy*, Vol. 33, no. 1, spring 1988, pp.63-80; Paul Fueter, "Confessing Christ Through Liturgy: An Orthodox Challenge to Protestants", *Lutheran World*, Vol. 23, no. 3, 1976, pp.180-86.

8. Theodore Stylianopoulos, "Jesus Christ — The Life of the World: A Christological Reflection", in *Orthodox Contributions to the Vancouver Theme*, Geneva, WCC, 1982, p.31.

9. Cf. *Your Kingdom Come*, pp. 203f.